World Trends and Cultural Power

Seven Experts on the Near Future

By: D. V. Poole, Bruce Piasecki
and Lt.Col. Robin Noel Phillips

With:
Dr. Zabihollah Rezaee,
Dr. Larry Clay Jr., Dennis J. Easter MBA,
and Dr. W. Keith Story

Copyright © 2025 by Creative Force Foundation, Inc.

All rights reserved. This book or any portion thereof may not be reproduced or used in any manner whatsoever without the express written permission of the publisher except for the use of brief quotations in a book review.

ISBN: 979-8-35097-978-7 (print)
ISBN: 979-8-35097-979-4 (eBook)

Acknowledgments

Many exceptional people are behind this effort. Key amongst them and without whose constant support and overview this book could not have been written:

Mr. Edward M. Frazer
Lt. Col. Robin Noel Phillips
Brig. Gen. Clara M.L. Adams-Ender
George W. Brown, J.D. *(d.)* & Evelyn White Brown
Kathleen W. Gallon, M.A.
Derrick A. Humphries, J.D.
Edward & Harriet Kotomori
Trent A. L. Poole, M.S.
Martin "Mickey" Reiss, P.E.
and Ted M. Winestone, J.D., CPA *(d.)*

TABLE OF CONTENTS

Chapter One: Overview and Declaration of Intentions
Darryl Vernon Poole 1

Chapter Two: The Ark of Power and the Way to Tomorrow
Lt. Colonel Robin Noel Phillips, United States Army (Ret.) 11

Chapter Three: Navigating the New Paradigm: Stakeholder Capitalism and Governance of Sustainability
Zabihollah (Zabi) Rezaee 47

Chapter Four: Our Quantum Moment in History: Bridging Education Gaps and Introducing the Future of Leadership and Management towards Human Flourishing
Dr. Larry Clay Jr. 77

Chapter Five: What Does a Solutions Engineer Do with Electronic Reporting Platforms in Smaller and Mid-Size Firms?
Dennis J. Easter 98

Chapter Six: Managing the Supply Chain of Our Turbulent and Changing World: The Next Steps
W. Keith Story 147

Chapter Seven: What Robin Hood Tells Us About Confronting the Climate Crisis (and Other World Trends)
By Bruce Piasecki 173

Chapter Eight: Finale: Advice and Cascading Links
D.V. Poole 194

Appendix: Top 90 World Trends Books at Your Side - a Short Further Readings 'Crash List'
Works helping to inform our collective "Sense of the Near Future" as Selected over a 50-Year period by D.V. Poole. 201

Limited Endnotes:
Critical World Trends and Combined Cultural Power: What Experts Are Finding Out About the Near Future 209

Chapter One

Overview and Declaration of Intentions

Darryl Vernon Poole

Welcome to 2026….*and beyond 2030*.

I initiated this collection to begin transferring lessons learned from working with an amazing set of practitioners, applied researchers, and authors for many years. These six dedicated people always struck me and many others as particularly informed, prepared, compassionate, and focused on excellence. In addition to being highly professional, they hold deep concerns for our shared, pressing futures, and join me in an effort to transfer our life lessons to those who will follow and achieve more.

Our intention is to share observations we earned by watching world trends and cultural developments from a variety of security desks, corporate positions, and government positions. We call this a collective sharing of a "world trends plateau" earned through more than 320 years of combined work experience and constant, task driven, on-the-ground observations. As a plateau, this anthology offers you a set of vistas, not peaks…a framework, rather than an agenda.

Why would we want to share with you such a pragmatic applied and humanistic anthology?

First, we have observed across *very different careers* what can float to the top of complex organizations as cream rather than sludge. We have had to solve unusual problems while resolving endemic conflicts. We have deliberately placed our observations thus gained into tightly worded tactical summaries for you. The following sequence of eight chapters opens with the most challenging opportunity we face, and ends with the hopes that we can achieve this and more … and why.

Second, you share in both message and chapter, content and world trends in this collection; all are meant for the next generations of professionals and good people including: *(a.)* deans of business, law, diplomacy, and military sciences who must determine the direction of education, as well as find and choose those who can teach for the future rather than the present, *(b.)* current leaders of the traumas and achievements of the present as well as sculptors of the future, and *(c.)* you, who must lead—ready or not—those "inheritors" who are about to follow as well to take the reins that we are charged to pass.

Third, as a reader of this collection, you will need to help your leaders use and adapt these pragmatic observations to governments, business enterprises, and social organizations. In an ever-changing world, some of these messages can float to the top of your organization and career over time. But you must update each message for your specific circumstances.

Using the collective knowledge in this book is not a one-time read; it is much more a process, an aid, if you will, to help increase your own situational diagnoses. This requires contemplation, consideration, and then action. Come back to this collection as you ascend through different stages of your career.

Who Are We?

Over the last half century, my work has been about the sequential convergence of critical global and domestic factors. For decades, I served as a corporate staff director, and later as CFO for several smaller-sized entities. Thereafter, I steered a unique international research network while for nine years producing the private executive letter, *Institute Commentaries on World Change* (recognized by National Library of Congress under *ISSN-1555-2349*), summing up monthly world trends-beneath-trends for key leaders.

That body of work provided alerts to corporations, governments, and leaders directly, drawing consistently upon facts – separate from opinions – that are relentlessly driving:

* Planetary climate and regional weather conditions

* Expansion of what constitutes warfare

* Embracing of uncivil wars rather than conflict resolution

* Acceptance of frighteningly high human collateral damage

* Famine, both regional and broadening across the world

* Plagues and related world epidemics, now widely noted in the press

* World-wide rejections of formerly understood democratic processes

* Systemic corrosion in what constitutes leadership

* How the drive for institutional, ideological, or even individual power has been replaced by an open lust for personal power

* Collapse of health care systems

* Erosion of governance & legal systems (see the chapter by Zabi on trust, integrity, probity, reliance, justiciability, effectiveness)

* Profound rise in corruption, income inequalities, and closely held wealth.

This represents a dozen accelerating, conflicting, and converging elements in both domestic and global business and society.

The common thread: in short, all of the above led to the accretion of unshared power which cannot be simply fixed, but it can be better understood, balanced, and better aligned for the future by stronger collective and collaborative actions.

> *(For an idea of how extensive these world trends came about and extend into your life and your family and friends, please see the published list of the more important books on these world trends at the end of this Anthology. We list them at the end as our conclusion, and the notes assembled for further reading.)*

Together with my coauthors in this anthology, we are a collection of seven relatively ordinary doers and original thinkers. Even more have shared my 90-books referenced in our closing chapter, yet synthesized our own ways and applications across our decades-long careers.

Our combined training and experiences include the following fields:

Audit, Accounting, and Finance	Consulting & Private Advisory
Complex Change Management	Governance

Federal Government Governance & Executive Leadership Human Resources Management	Geology Academic Institutions of Higher Learning Institution & Organization Governance
Defense Career Military Branches Nursing & Health Care Private & Public Manufacturing State & Local Governments	NGO & Non-Profit Management Planning & Control Research & Intelligence Public & Private Professional Services

We do share some odd traits, which got us all together. We all have led pragmatic operations. We were promoted to senior management roles. We then chose to teach people—those upcoming in the ranks. In addition, we collected and advised in earnest a select few who clearly wanted to achieve more than just a career (in both academic and business settings) or a just a livelihood. We helped ready some of these people who, having served and advised high positions of governance, had chosen to undertake task-driven professional lives. We have observed all this across several operational generations. So now we look back, and reflect for the sake of sharing forward the better of what has been learned. You must mentor yourselves as well, using these words and frameworks to define your tasks.

There is another oddity in this collection of writers. While we either hold or have held various professional certifications, licenses, general and advanced degrees, none of us are merely theoreticians. Across the course of very different individual careers, we have had to either solve hard, complicated problems "instantly," or face increasingly difficult decisions. We learned how to deliver on both strategic and tactical planning, then implement immediate or lasting solutions to defend the interests of our country on foreign soil. We do not reveal these international secrets we shared, instead we focus on world trends that you can see if you dig deep enough in the evidence and cultural debris before you.

Like most of our readers, each of us was primarily hired to *"get things DONE."* Each of us was hired to offer action and advice, agendas and value. Yet we all value practice over theory, historic truth and facts over method and dispute.

Politically, we represent full spectrum. By 2025, this eclectic combination renders our conclusions and individual focus points more urgent: for the welfare of our multiple societies, we must find, move to, and adapt to "common ground." Long ago, Bruce Piasecki wrote a book titled <u>In Search of Environmental Excellence</u>. The core truth within that book lay in its subtitle: *"Moving Beyond Blame."* That is one of the critical tones we have adopted for this book.

It may come as a surprise, but individually, none of us sees the world in quite the same way. It is more appropriate to view the world as a set of converging trends. Yet each of us in this collection has been shaped by a belief in the founding missions and purposes of the United States of America. Over the course of our lives, we have seen how many of these purposes have been globalized in large segments of other nations. Examples like aviation and higher education have worked wonders for the world. There are other ramifications of solutions in the world of big data and the internet.

Thus, this is an anthology of hope, as well as a reflection on world trends, to be remembered and mastered by watching and reflecting on how the American tradition has been globalized.

Why We Wrote This Book

On the cover of Dr. Roman Krznaric's book, THE GOOD ANCESTOR, there is a dedicatory quote from the late Jonas Salk: **"The most important question we must ask ourselves is, 'Are we being good ancestors?'"**

Sometime during the middle of the Coronavirus-19 pandemic and into the present endemic, my fellow coauthors and I began to share thoughts with each other on our global conditions. There emerged a growing concern for how later generations would inherit our problems (say, 50 years from now), and answer them. What would they say to, or ask of, us? How would they see us? Would it be for what we accomplished? Or for what we failed to provide for our own inheritors?

To begin, we believe there are still grounds for hope and reform. So far, violent bickering and a focus on popular but short-term issues have not produced legacies of self-sacrifice, collective determination, or the forward momentum required for real progress. Consider climate change, which Dr. Piasecki and others first wrote about in 1990, over a third of a century ago. Think about war, and the consequences of war and poverty, written about by many in the appendix. These all seem daunting. And yet, a path to solutions is open to the new generations, more than ever.

We further noted that what we are seeing are not political problems, but universally repeating problems found across all histories. We will show a number of examples of this throughout the book. At its best, a good anthology is a smart toolbox, one that attempts to empower the immediate generations, rather than saddling them with the constant job of fixing broken wheels.

So, as a cadre of "get the damn job done" careerists what would we say now? What short messages in a bottle would we – given the opportunity – wish most to hand back to the next generations?

We decided to lean back from our strong individual opinions and join hands, agreeing with the tone of Daniel Patrick Forrester's 2011 book title suggesting to just CONSIDER. Doing this required considering four coordinating questions, four corners to our World:

- **What do we do with** this?
- **What have we** learned?
- **Where are we most** troubled?
- **Where do we find** Hope?

To do this, we further concluded that we must speak primarily from the *heart* rather than our combined *intellects*; but this Anthology includes both.

We also must speak from an individual and combined level of Hope.

For your own careers, simply treat these combined messages as signal flares and banners of profound opportunities for excellence. We focus our attention on what can be achieved. Hope is a real thing, when pragmatic and action orientated; it is the opposite of wishful thinking. The time to act on these frameworks is now. Each of us has four Great Powers enabling us to make positive changes in the world:

- **The power to** convene
- **The power to** observe
- **The power to** believe
- **The power to choose to do** good

Consider this Anthology an addendum to what Herman Khan, Eleanor Roosevelt, George Washington, John F. Kennedy, Dorothy Irene Height, all perceived in their working lives, as reported in history. Read these essays as coming from **"We, the PEOPLE…"** Why? Because we *ARE* the People to which the document refers!

In a nutshell, here is the message of this Anthology: Those who manage the delivery and implementation of solutions are now urged to get beyond blame in little things, and work on the big things before business and society. We need to sacrifice short-term selfishness for a greater and increasing need for long-term goals and perspectives.

Prepare to address some of these questions head on now. Read with an eye to "THE NEXT STEPS" you may have to take to understand the future you will manage, and in which you must be prepared to lead. By corresponding with these authors and others, perhaps you will be better prepared to offer more specific recommendations covering what we all are facing between now and 2030, along with specific actions and steps the newer generations will need to take to improve upon the conditions we are passing back to them.

One Last Item Before You Begin

Why release this a book targeted for 2026, well after a year marked by a record number of national-level elections around the globe, affecting nearly half the world's population? Simple: we foresaw that the year 2024 would be seen as a year of turbulence and big pivots, with much more global resonance in one year than the last decade combined. Regardless of all this turbulence, we believe the new under-45 generations will still need to choose the right ponds to swim in for their (or your) own growth, maturity, risks, and successes.

Well beyond 2026, we want you all to carry some of these forthcoming observations forward, exclaiming to those you must train, mentor, nurture and develop: *"Here's what we have observed. Here's what we can do now to advance past these inherited trends and problems."* What we offer now is a short, compressed summary of many prior observations first left in dozens of books, publications and speeches. By providing these small transparent bottles, we leave it to you to make it actionable now.

Despite our litany of difficulties stated above, *"We, the People..."* in this and other countries **are still characterized as a uniquely resilient, and very human, resource.** Many in our midst, like some of these chapter authors, have the capacity for individual conscience and collective compassion. In a sense, despite the challenges faced in our work, our community helped reinforce our individual efforts over the decades.

This is what remains for your unpuzzling: Our toughest remaining human challenge seems to be the ability to know when, how, and for what better purpose we can rapidly use gifts already abundant in our species. Book writing is a start, but your actions over time are what matter most.

***Darryl Vernon Poole*, November 2024**

Chapter Two

The Ark of Power and the Way to Tomorrow

Lt. Colonel Robin Noel Phillips,
United States Army (Ret.)

The Coming Collapse: How Did We Get Here? Where Are We Going?

You may call it a cataclysm, a disaster, or a catastrophe. For some decades now, I have thought of it as "the coming collapse." This "it", of course, is climate change, and all of the ramifications that it brings to every aspect of human society and civilization.

Thirty to forty years ago, there seemed to be few everyday people who took climate change seriously enough for a thoughtful conversation. In an age when globalization was on the upswing, consumer goods were cheaper and more accessible than ever, and exotic fresh foods from around the world became available year-round. Life seemed good. It was easy to believe that climate change wasn't real, to rationalize that it was not a big problem, or that if it were, human ingenuity would prevail.

Not anymore. There is a growing sense, especially among younger generations, of this coming collapse. People are increasingly worried about patterns of change that can no longer be denied or wished away. Derelict fishing ships lie in a desert that was once the Aral Sea. Temperate-zone lakes and ponds where families once ice skated no longer freeze over. Aquifers are physically collapsing in the western United States, ruined, never again to contain water. On the other side of the world in Delhi, India, many people's taps have run dry, and they must purchase water – often non-potable water – that is trucked into their neighborhoods.

These are the multiplying consequences of a set of interconnected, global-scale changes in environment and climate. They are just the tip of the iceberg, and they are fast-moving. Everything mentioned in the above paragraph was wrought by human activity, and it has all happened in *less than one human* lifetime.

We are living during what I believe to be *the* most unusual time in human history, characterized by a number of factors never seen before:

- A truly global economy that is more responsive to consumer demand.
- The highest global literacy rates in human history
- Technological and scientific advances on an unprecedented scale and pace of evolution.
- An accelerating pace of accumulation of human knowledge.
- The means for people anywhere in the world to communicate almost instantaneously with each other.
- An *enormous, unnatural, and unsustainable peak in the human population,* made possible by scientific advances, driven further

by technological achievements, but now threatens to bring all of those down under its own weight.

For the purposes of discussion, I consider this "most unusual time in human history" to begin around the mid-nineteenth century, when advances in agricultural production massively increased crop yields and drove a sharp upward spike in human population. One might be forgiven for thinking that, thanks to our human ingenuity, we had embarked upon a Golden Age of limitless potential for humankind. But this was never going to last; we have been overdrawing our resources at unsustainable rates. The signs are becoming ever more apparent that the wave that brought us to this peak is beginning to break and crash. It is important to understand our era – *the era of peak population* – as extremely new, relatively short, and temporary.

It is finally dawning upon us that the Earth and its resources are finite; our activity is unquestionably changing the environment in ways that present various threats now and for a significant time to come; and our many achievements have carried the seeds of their own undoing, and perhaps ours. Our advances in industrial-scale agricultural practices have resulted in food that is less nutritious than it was 50 years ago, and have introduced hormones and pesticides that threaten our health. The invention of antibiotics was a Godsend for medicine, but the way we overuse them has resulted in antibiotic-resistant diseases. The rapidly accelerating expansion of total human knowledge, as it turns out, includes vast amounts of factually wrong, hateful, or misguided social media content that stifles intellectual curiosity and promotes divisiveness and unrest. Much of our modern way of life – not just in the United States, but all over the world – depends on non-renewable petroleum products, which are inherently unsustainable, and contribute to environmental degradation and rapid climate change that we are ill-prepared to face.

We are past the tipping point and unable or unwilling to cooperate sufficiently to reverse it. So the questions now are:

- How can we best understand the threat of climate change in order to better prepare for it?
- What can we do to minimize human suffering?
- What can we do to maintain human advances, progress, and civilization?
- What can we do to assure the survival of the human species, both short-term and long-term?

For all of our human shortcomings, we still have immense potential. If the negative aspects of human nature have contributed to this crisis point in our history, then identifying and leveraging our more positive characteristics will help us successfully weather the next several centuries, and come out the other side with our civilization as intact as possible.

The future is never a certainty, but by examining human history, planetary history, and ongoing trends, we can make some educated predictions about how we got to this point, and what we are likely to face in the next century or two.

Trends, Trajectories, and Timing

Over the next century or so, we will see escalating, complex, and inter-related trends affecting the climate, the environment, political borders, and relations between groups of people – whether those groups are defined by nation, ethnic group, race, wealth, social status, or religion.

I categorize these trends into four major inter-related challenges that we will face:

- **Climate and Environmental Change**
- **Population**
- **Resource Depletion**
- **Awareness of and Response to the Crisis**

We are gifted with the ability to observe these trends, to define their trajectories, and to determine whether the trends, if continued, present a danger to the human species. If so, we have the capacity to act in ways to alter these trajectories toward a more favorable outcome for ourselves.

Climate and Environmental Change

More and more people now agree that rapid climate change is real, and that it presents potentially catastrophic challenges for human populations. However, there is still argument – even among scientists – over the extent to which human activity contributes to the phenomenon. The truth is, there are two major influences at work on climate change: long-term, geological and astronomical patterns that drive cyclical climate change over many millennia; and human activity that is driving rapid climate change. In addition to climate change, there are the separate but closely related issues of environmental degradation and resource depletion, which are overwhelmingly driven by human activity.

Long-Term Geological Environmental Change: The Next 100,000 Years and Beyond

Separate from human-driven factors, there is a larger, still poorly understood geological phenomenon that proceeds cyclically and inexorably far beyond our influence. Our climate is affected in part by the precession of the Earth's axis, as well as subtle variations in Earth's orbit around the Sun. It can also be altered swiftly and catastrophically by normal geological processes or occasional collisions with celestial objects. Even if we could reverse the human impact on climate, we cannot stave off long-term climate change on a geological and astronomical scale. What we can do is overcome our false sense of permanence to recognize it, and prepare ourselves to adapt to it.

Ice Ages and Interglacials

If humans are to survive long-term – *very* long-term – we must be able to adapt to drastic climate change. Over the past 800,000 years or so, the Earth has cycled through a series of glacial periods, or ice ages, interspersed with interglacial periods characterized by warmer temperatures and retreat of the glaciers (although they generally don't disappear entirely). During an ice age, sea levels drop significantly; during the interglacials, sea levels rise, sometimes much more rapidly than they are rising today. The change in sea level can be extreme; this is why mastodon fossils can be found on the Continental Shelf, and marine fossils can be found on the American Great Plains.

Glacial periods have typically lasted between 70,000 years and 90,000 years. Interglacials are shorter, typically around 10,000 years. The interglacial that we are currently living in is already unusually long, at about 11,000 years. This long duration will likely play a key role in the extent of melting of the world's glaciers.

The longer our planet remains under warm interglacial conditions, the more of our glacial ice will melt and the more sea level will rise. Our current, unusually long interglacial appears likely to persist, thanks to the warming trend produced by human activities. Some climate scientists believe this trend could last as long as 150,000 years, essentially "skipping" the next glacial period. The longer our high temperatures persist, the more ice will melt, and the more land will eventually be inundated.

What might this look like? Geological data from the last interglacial, around 125,000 years ago, show that the average global temperature then was about 3 degrees Celsius higher than it is today. Sea level reached 30 meters higher than present sea level. Whether one meter, three meters, 30 meters, or more, a steep sea level rise will be devastating to coastal populations and low-lying island nations. Inundation is only the most obvious threat; there will also be seawater contamination of reservoirs and aquifers near the coast, loss of agricultural lands, and all of the social, political, and cultural impacts of the forced migration of countless environmental refugees competing with other populations for shrinking land and resources.

Sudden and Unpredictable Global Catastrophes

The cycles of climate change, with their rising and falling temperatures and sea levels, are not the only existential threats we face. There are also global catastrophes that occur in a number of ways:

- Major astronomical catastrophes, such as asteroid and meteor strikes
- Coronal Mass Ejection (CME) events, solar bursts from the sun, which given our reliance on electrical and electronic devices for just about everything, could wreak havoc on everything from transportation to banking to water supplies
- Large volcanic eruptions such as the 1883 eruption of Krakatoa.
- Man-made catastrophes such as nuclear war or meltdowns at nuclear stations.

We are already struggling to mitigate or adapt to the immediate effects of rapid, short-term climate change over the next few hundred years. Any one of these geological, astronomical, or man-made catastrophes would instantly tip us over the edge into a full-blown emergency of exploding famine, disease, mass migrations, and all of the conflict and destruction that historically follows upon such conditions.

**Short-Term, Human-Influenced Environmental Change:
The Next 100 – 500 Years**

If we are to think productively about very long-term human survival, our first task is to survive the Coming Collapse and the next 100-500 years.

While one might argue the extent of human influence on the climate, there can no longer be any doubt that it is a significant factor. Since the early 20th century, scientists have suspected that the burning of fossil fuels and production of carbon dioxide would drive unnatural global temperature increases. Since the mid-20th century, they have been certain of it, and began warning the US Government of the probable long-term environmental consequences. Only now, well into the 21st century and with those environmental changes materializing before our eyes, are we finally beginning to take those warnings seriously.

Population and Resource Depletion

My father lived for 89 years, and in his lifetime, he saw the global human population triple. If I live as long as he did, I will see it triple in my lifetime as well. This is unprecedented in all of human history.

Although it is taboo in some circles to say so, our vast human population is absolutely the single largest factor driving rapid environmental change. It is only logical that more people will consume more of every resource. In simple terms, the amount of damage by any measurement one wishes is driven by the amount of activity, and the amount of activity is directly riven by the size and consumption of the human populations.

One does not have to look far for some disheartening examples. While I lament the impending losses of majestic creatures like rhinos or tigers or elephants, humankind should be much more alarmed to consider that already, one-quarter to one-third of freshwater fish are at risk of extinction. In the past 100 years, 80% of the biomass of ocean fish has been lost in an accelerating trend of overfishing; 60% of the biomass has been lost in the last 40 years alone.

The industrial-scale agriculture necessary to feed the human population is overdrawing our aquifers faster than they can recover. Once depleted, most of these large aquifers will not recover for hundreds or even thousands of years due to their slow recharge rates and the vast capacity that needs to be replenished. If an aquifer physically collapses, as is happening in the American West currently, its capacity to contain water is permanently destroyed.

Many have reminded me that in developed nations, our consumer excesses produce a much larger carbon footprint. This is true, but environmental change is not only about carbon and climate. It is about sustainability of resources. Farmers, fishermen, and herdsmen in developing nations destroy wildlife habitat, deplete soil nutrients, overgraze lands, deplete fish and wildlife populations, and overuse water resources. Everywhere and at every level, human beings do what they can to survive and thrive, at whatever environmental cost necessary. More people means more consumption at every level.

Our technological prowess has bought us time, but it has not stopped us from overdrawing our resources. Every solution brings its own environmental costs and trade-offs. We're not going to "technology our way out of this" by sheer force of will.

We are living in a vast, but closed, system called Planet Earth. It seems obvious that in any closed system, the key to surviving well is balance. When any animal population constantly grows, the population will inevitably outrun its available resources, and crash. As food and water resources recover, the remnants of the animal population can then recover as well. This repeating cycle is well documented and accepted when we are talking about deer or wolves in a limited space, but too few of us seem to consider that the laws of nature apply equally to the human species within the confines of the planet.

The current environmental cost to support the human population is incredibly high simply because there are so many of us. While wealthy countries undeniably generate far greater carbon emissions than poorer countries, all of us are contributing to the depletion of critical resources like potable water, natural habitats, fossil fuels, and food sources.

According to the Global Footprint Network, as of 2024, the overall global population is using natural resources and polluting the environment 1.7 times faster than the planet's capacity to regenerate. Ordinary, well-meaning people cannot significantly offset this destructive consumption by eating lab-grown meat, or turning down their thermostats, or buying electric vehicles, or taking shorter showers. Unseen by most of us, the major industries – without which we cannot survive in our billions – will continue to use up our natural resources on an enormous scale and will continue to contribute to rapid environmental change, at least for the next few decades; but the impact of our activities will persist for decades or centuries beyond that, and in some cases – like the physical collapse of major aquifers – the impact will last forever. We are permanently reducing the availability of critical resources not only for ourselves, but for all future generations. We are permanently reducing the carrying capacity of the Earth.

We now face a period of perhaps 100-500 years of painful adjustment to changing environmental conditions and availability of resources. I expect that within this time frame, our population will necessarily decline – through some combination of choice, conflict, climate effects, and deprivation - to a fraction of its current level.

Historians of the post-peak population era may very well look back upon the mid-19th century to the mid-22nd century as a remarkable anomaly of unsustainable population levels leading to unsustainable consumption, consequential disaster, and eventual recovery. The undetermined variables are the timing of the peak, the rate of population decline, and the level at which the population will eventually stabilize. This trajectory and outcome will be influenced by choices made by individuals and by government and religious leaders, as well as external factors like climate extremes, lack of basic resources, conflicts, disease, or catastrophic events.

Timing the Population Wave vs. Resource Depletion

Earth is facing an extremely uncertain and difficult period ahead. Amid climate shifts that have reached levels incompatible with human existence in some regions, our global population continues to rise while our resources are noticeably declining.

Timing is one of the most significant factors shaping the environment that we will face over the next century or so: the later our peak population occurs, the more we will have outrun our resources, and the more likely we are to see extensive deprivation and human suffering.

If we can allow our population to decline naturally by choice – the kindest course of action – we may be able to maximize resources and minimize human suffering.

Even a voluntary decline in population presents hardships, but until we reach a stage in which our population is right-sized and sustainably distributed for available land and resources, we will face considerable uncertainty, instability, conflict, and deprivation.

Awareness of and Response to the Climate Crisis

Awareness of the environmental threats we face is finally reaching a point of significant public interest, engagement, and mitigation efforts. Many news sources now devote an entire section to climate issues. Depletion of vital resources – especially water – is now widely recognized as reaching catastrophic levels. There is better public awareness of the importance of biodiversity. Many governments, nonprofits, and individuals increasingly recognize damage to the environment – at least, insofar as it affects us negatively – and have taken positive steps like requiring control of emissions or effluents, cleaning up rivers or toxic waste dumps, or protecting endangered species. New methods are being developed to recycle more plastics or to integrate non-recyclable plastics into building materials or pavements. There is greater investment in clean energy sources; the first vehicles powered by hydrogen fuel cells are now on the market in several countries. Public pressure on governments, manufacturers, and agricultural companies has given rise to the reporting of Environmental, Social, and Governance (ESG) metrics as a measure of corporate responsibility in these areas. Especially since the turn of the 21st century, many new organizations solely focused on sustainability are appearing.

Progress is never steady or in a straight line. There are still those who deny climate change, minimize the threat, or simply don't care. As government administrations change, rules fall by the wayside. More natural areas are opened to resource exploitation. Protections lapse. Pollution, once cleaned up, begins anew. Promises to curb the mining and burning of fossil fuels go unfulfilled. As described in Dr. Zabihollah Rezaee's extensive works on corporate sustainability, governance, and ethics, businesses too often find ways to fraudulently "greenwash" their ESG metrics.

Much of our progress, or lack of it, depends on the choices of the major players in the world today: sovereign governments, and large corporations. Their choices will likely have the greatest effects on the course that unfolds over the next 100-500 years.

Cooperation vs. Competition : Making Cooperation Our Priority

An enormous factor in our ability to respond to the climate crisis will hinge on the degree to which we either cooperate or compete.

Sovereign governments and large corporations are the dominant entities that engage in exploration, resource exploitation, manufacturing, energy production, building of infrastructure, large scale research, and wars. They compete with each other in these spheres, or cooperate through treaties and partnerships. Smaller business entities, local governments, nongovernmental organizations, nonprofits and individuals are subject to their laws and regulations. With few exceptions, their purchasing power is unmatched.

How the world's governments and corporations respond to current and future events will not appreciably alter the immediate course of rapid climate change – we have missed that boat. But it is still possible to plan and act in ways to minimize human suffering, increase the chances that the human species will adapt to our new environment, and ensure that our civilization will survive not only for the next several centuries, but for millennia thereafter.

The question is, can the world's governments and corporations cooperate internationally to achieve the best possible outcome for everyone? Or will they continue to compete aggressively for dwindling resources and create shortsighted policies?

Let's look at this issue at the national and international levels.

At the National Level

Before a nation can be effective in the international arena, it must be internally stable and have populations capable of cooperating internally. Unfortunately, in recent years, we have seen increasing popular dissatisfaction and political divisiveness around the world, hobbling our collective ability to cooperate on a strategic scale.

A significant portion of the dissatisfaction is focused on cultural friction arising from migrations of large numbers of refugees into host nations with a markedly different cultural character than the migrants, creating a perception that the migrants threaten their host nations' cultures, economies, or security, or take resources from local populations.

Another major source of popular dissatisfaction, at least in the United States, is a very real and increasing insufficiency of the middle class. People with ostensibly good education and decent jobs find themselves making tough financial choices, especially concerning higher education, home ownership, and healthcare. The perception is that too many middle-class citizens are facing growing difficulty making ends meet, even in two-income households, while the CEOs they work for are making more than 300 times as much as their front-line workers.

This dissatisfaction will likely grow stronger as resources become scarcer. Thanks to the global economy and advanced agricultural technology, adults in their prime today have always enjoyed wide selections of relatively cheap consumer goods and year-round access to foods from around the world: shrimp from Bangladesh, grapes from Chile. Like our population spike, we are likely near the peak of this temporary phenomenon driven by rapid and unsustainable use of our resources. In coming decades, due to both resource depletion and rising energy costs for manufacturing and transport, the availability of cheap goods and affordable foods from distant sources will likely decline.

Also, resources flow to the markets that can pay. Even as the average citizen loses consumer choices and purchasing power, CEOs and billionaires will be able to maintain their lifestyle longer than the rest of us.

This is a national security issue; it is what revolutions are made of. No one revolts because someone else has yachts, vacation homes, and private jets. They revolt because someone else has those things, while they – ostensibly with a well-paying job – are forced to choose between rent and their child's lifesaving insulin. They revolt not because of mere inequity, but because of that inequity *and* their own insufficient resources to simply live.

The danger in an enraged public provoked into "tearing it all down" is that there are always unintended consequences and destruction of human progress. Climate change will bring its own challenges to national stability, so now more than ever, it is imperative that national leaders promote conditions for cooperation and innovation.

International Competition

Even the most cursory review of human history reveals a long succession of wars, conquests, and genocides. There is only so much land and ocean upon which to survive civilizations must either expand to incorporate by either peaceful, cultural and/or violent means. This history of international competition continues to play out to the present day in terms of hyper-competitive economics – or what we consider to be globally interactive business enterprises.

Most businesses compete for profit rather than operating for long-term sustainability. For example, energy companies in the United States use fracking to extract fossil fuels, despite the resulting permanent destruction of aquifers on which local residents depend. Cotton growers in Central Asia destroyed the Aral Sea, and its fish populations, by diverting water to their crops. Oil companies in Venezuela, and the Venezuelan government, have allowed a decrepit oil infrastructure to destroy Lake Maracaibo, its aquatic life, and the health and livelihoods of residents in the region. India and China, the world's two most populous nations, continue to depend heavily, and unapologetically, upon coal as a major source of energy to modernize their economies and raise the standard of living for more than one-quarter of the world's population. And at the United Nations climate summit in late 2023, oil-producing nations resisted any action to cut production of fossil fuels, citing the need to protect people's livelihoods. There are many other examples around the world that demonstrate again and again that governments and corporations cannot, or will not, cooperate well enough to meet the environmental threats of the next century.

Although our species is wired for both cooperation and competition within our tribes and between groups, human nature primes us to take care of ourselves and those most closely associated with us first, to the detriment of those who are not. The fewer resources there are to go around, the more pressure there is to compete, rather than cooperate. The upshot is that all conflicts are really about resource competition. While I agree with Samuel Huntington's premise that people's religious and cultural identities will be the main fault lines along which conflicts occur, I maintain that conflict is *not* truly about religion, or race, or nationality; those are merely the markers that we choose to divide "us" from "them. " The closer one group physically is to another, the more direct is their competition for the same resources. Resources might be land, water, food, hunting / fishing grounds, mates, or even things like education, employment, power, status, influence, access—ANYTHING that confers an advantage is a resource. Even ancestral homelands may be thought of as a physical resource. Let any resource get scarce enough, and competition is ascendant.

A competitive scenario in coming decades could take the form of resource hoarding, countries waging war to gain access to resources, and governments enacting policies to preserve or increase their own populations to gain a numerical advantage, or as an attempt to preserve their economies at current levels. A scenario like this will increase human suffering, waste scarce resources, and degrade the environment even further.

As basic resources such as food and water become scarcer, they will tend to flow to markets that can pay; marginalized groups will suffer and die first and in the greatest numbers. Migration due to land loss and extreme weather will increase localized competition for declining resources and will provoke ever more conflict in a vicious cycle. People will become increasingly desperate for survival; look for extinction of more large species in the wild as they lose habitat or water sources, or are killed for meat, and look for incidents of human genocide as groups seek to eliminate competition. Unless governments take action, maternal and infant mortality will rise due to poor access to food, potable water, and proper care, and rising rates of disease. This will tend to contribute to the downward trend in our numbers.

We can see these things happening already. For example, in 2023, the United Nations reports that 26% of the world's people have no access to the most basic amenity for survival: safe drinking water. That is a raging alarm bell.

International Cooperation

In a cooperative scenario, however, the next century might see vast changes in how we educate and train the next generation for a tumultuous period of adaptation to a new environmental reality.

This approach would be emotionally, politically, and logistically arduous. It would require intense focus, thoughtful and cooperative planning based on the best available data, and highly effective strategic communication with the public. But it would be possible.

Governments could plan in advance to relocate those who will be affected by sea level rise or extreme temperatures. If global population declines as quickly as predicted near the end of the 21st century, there would likely be available housing or even entire towns which could be repurposed for the benefit of environmental migrants. But this scenario assumes a high degree of popular willingness to accept relocation of citizens, immigration of new populations from abroad, cultural shifts, abandonment of former ways of life, and learning new languages, trades, and technologies as needs evolve.

This will be exquisitely difficult for everyone, but especially for cultures that particularly value ethnic homogeneity or people whose homelands will be completely lost.

The United Nations is actively engaged in work to define the extent of climate change threats and to propose actions to mitigate those threats. Organizations under UN auspices have clear goals focusing on food security, agriculture, potable water, poverty, and other factors linked to climate change. These organizations articulate steps needed to achieve meaningful steps toward mitigating these issues.

But routinely, the world's governments announce that we are falling short.

I am not optimistic that the human species can execute a cooperative scenario. We have appropriate organizations, knowledge, and policies in place, but we also have an abysmal track record of using these advantages effectively, if at all.

In a best-case scenario, enough of us will unite our efforts to cooperate and find solutions enabling the human species to adapt to the environmental changes that are coming. In a worst-case scenario, we will see intensifying competition for dwindling resources, which will only serve to magnify conflicts, disease, loss of natural resources and human suffering. As with all real-world events, reality will fall somewhere in between. How it materializes will depend greatly on the choices that we all make.

Enabling Survival

Even facing the challenges ahead, I do not think that we will be extinct any time soon. The modern human species has existed for about 200,000 to 315,000 years, depending on which paleontologist you ask. Clearly, human beings – at least, tribes or small bands of them – can survive ice ages, global warming, and sea level rise.

But human *civilization*, marked by the rise of agriculture and the written word, has only existed for about 5,000 to 6,000 years, during a time of remarkably stable climate conditions. In this time frame, individual civilizations and empires have risen and fallen. Human population collapses have occurred, and will happen again. Each time, humanity has lost some of the knowledge and progress gained by those civilizations.

Human civilization has never faced environmental change on the sheer scale that we are facing now, nor have we ever had such an enormous population competing for shrinking planetary resources. Our own, probably inconsistent, future behavior is a variable that introduces significant uncertainty into the overall situation.

Trying to stem the tide of human-influenced environmental change is like trying to turn an aircraft carrier. It requires a long lead time that we no longer have. Trying to stem the tide of geological and astronomical processes is far beyond our current abilities. But that does not mean we should do nothing.

In whatever way we can slow down the process of human-influenced climate change, we should. In whatever way we can preserve a global environment in which we can thrive, we should. In whatever way we can prepare ourselves to thrive for millennia to come, we should – and that means being able to adapt to extreme conditions, even beyond today's worst-case scenarios for global warming.

If you don't remember anything else about this essay, remember this:

- *Adaptation is key to survival.*
- *Diversity is key to adaptation.*

Over the course of its history, our planet's environment has always drastically changed. Temperatures, gas proportions, volcanism, radiation, plate tectonic upheavals, ocean composition, and aridity all have significantly altered over time. The occasional large-scale volcanic eruptions, major asteroid or meteor impacts have been responsible for further abrupt an extreme life support condition.

For most species to adapt to environmental change, there must be enough genetic diversity among their individuals so that some will be able to survive the new conditions, and even thrive.

Humans may experience genetic adaptation to a hotter world. Possibly those who are more resilient in response to disease, or who are physically more tolerant of heat or famine, will have a survival edge. But humankind is also able to adapt to threats and changing conditions by using two of our greatest advantages: the power of intellect, and the power of complex and abstract language – especially written language which can transmit information across many generations. Diversity plays a role in adaptation and survivability here, too: the diversity of culture, ideas, and innovations can confer a survival advantage in changing conditions.

In the last 5,000 to 6,000 years, we have not just survived, we have flourished. We have seen tremendous advances in art, recorded history, the sciences, and technology. This progress must not be lost. To carry the accomplishments of our civilization forward into the future, we must be able to adapt to extreme changes in our environment. To be able to adapt, we must retain as much diversity as possible, and we must have diversity of effort. Loss of progress, loss of decipherable information, and loss of biodiversity will make us less likely to survive.

There are those who believe humanity is facing extinction. It need not be thus. If we maintain our civilization and preserve the widest possible diversity of plant and animal species, we will vastly increase our chances of surviving the coming collapse and continuing to flourish on the other side of it. If we are successful, we can continue to build upon our current level of progress and adapt to future environmental change as it arises, enabling our species to thrive for many millennia to come.

Our immediate efforts must focus on bridging the crisis of falling human population numbers and climate-related social and political disruption that we are facing now and for the next 100-500 years. The best outcome we can hope for is that we collectively cooperate to realize a "bridge" effort to successfully reach a period of stability under new, as yet unknown, environmental conditions with our cumulative knowledge and progress as intact as possible.

Our tasks going forward from this point are clear:

- *Minimize human suffering.*
- *Maintain human advances, progress, and civilization.*
- *Assure the survival of the human species.*

Bridging the Next 100-500 Years

In any scenario, our overriding task must be to minimize human suffering. This is best addressed by governments, whose purpose is to create a stable, secure environment where their citizens can flourish. But certainly, all of us – corporations, nongovernmental organizations, nonprofits, and individuals – can and should cooperatively contribute.

We know that we are facing a period of increasing instability, so governments must start now to craft plans and policies in cooperation with think tanks, corporations, and climate and sustainability organizations. This will require science-based policies and efforts in anticipation of predictable future conditions and events, a tremendous amount of financial commitment, and well-considered public communication plans. All of us, in different professions, must recognize, articulate, and plan for rising needs in our areas of expertise. The totality of the effort is so complex that a large degree of specialization and innovation will be called for.

A generally agreed-upon way forward might address some of the following elements (this list is not exhaustive by any means):

Define the desired end state. The end state to achieve and maintain through this period of change should be a global population that has housing, access to potable water and sufficient food, is physically secure, and retains current educational and technological levels or better. We must preserve what we have now in terms of biodiversity, technology, information, and knowledge. This vision will be best achieved by minimizing conflicts and maximizing cooperation.

Strategic Communication is necessary to achieve buy-in from the public, to prioritize cooperation over competition, and to coordinate global efforts. One of the most important efforts we must undertake is to manage the expectations of a younger population. For example, prior to our current era of peak population and a global economy, food was historically much more expensive and difficult to obtain. It is essential to understand the reality that the past several decades of cheap fast food and cheap consumer goods has been an unsustainable aberration, not the norm.

Education: We must continue to promote science-based education for everyone, and empowerment of women globally. This will maximize availability of needed skills and specialties, as well as the innovation we will desperately need to meet the challenges we are facing.

Population must be allowed to fall by choice. One important goal for the future should be to reduce the human population over time through *voluntary* natural attrition. It is well documented that the single biggest thing anyone can do to reduce their carbon footprint is to have one less child. Draconian measures are not required; it is well documented that people everywhere will overwhelmingly choose to have fewer children, spaced farther apart, if they are educated and provided with the means to control their own reproduction.

As it happens, we may be on our way to that goal. New research shows that fertility is already dropping in many countries, largely due to personal choice. If the current trend in fertility continues, our population will continue to grow until the mid- to late 21st century, and then decline.

This trend comes too late to mitigate or avoid the immediate consequences of near-term climate change, but to maximize our resources, *it is exactly what we* need.

Policymakers and even climate scientists are loath to tackle the overpopulation issue head-on. Quite the opposite, governments and economists see a falling population as a problem to be solved.

We need to get away from the idea that a healthy economy needs to constantly grow. What is needed is balance, or a "right-sizing" of the economy and our resources to the population.

The more we can allow population to decline naturally by choice, the less it will have to decline through human suffering due to war, famine, or disease resulting from insufficient resources. A smaller global population, properly distributed, would have more resources to share, including residential and agricultural lands.

A disturbing macro-problem to solve is how would we get from 9 billion people down to 4 billion or 3 billion with the least possible negative consequences. Governments should craft plans and policies to coordinate a balanced economy, tax base, and services through a predicted period of declining birthrate, an aging global population, and the inevitable redistribution of populations which will occur over the next 100-500 years in the form of internal and international migrations and immigrant integration.

Workforce Structure: Governments and think tanks should be projecting and constantly updating demographic trends to predict and publicize the specialties that will be most in demand and, more importantly, most needed during the decades following peak population. Such a future could require a surge in engineers for infrastructure and materials reclamation, agricultural experts, social scientists, national security specialists, and innovators in the scientific and technological fields. There would also be a temporary surge, but then a decline, in the need for gerontologists and other age-related medical specialties. These projections should be publicly shared as part of any strategic communications or educational effort, and when needed, incentives should be offered to encourage people to fill positions in the most critically needed areas.

Migration Planning, Preparation, and Management: This brings us to perhaps the most difficult aspect of preparing to adapt and survive well over the next few centuries: managing the inevitable large-scale migrations that will certainly occur both nationally and internationally. Historically, mass migrations driven by survival have caused friction and conflict. Remember my point earlier that conflict, at its root, about competition for resources.

Today, we are already seeing many examples of the kinds of internal conflict that result from large numbers of immigrants from one culture migrating into countries of another culture. We will face a sharp increase in this phenomenon in the future. Governments, then, must craft policies and plans for internal migrations of their own citizens, and for integrating and resettling migrants.

Managing migration will be incredibly complex and difficult, but it need not be viewed as a problem or a threat; it is a powerful potential solution to falling fertility. Over the next century, as the global population falls, the governments that can thoughtfully integrate immigrants will have an advantage in terms of maintaining higher levels of human capital, and will be more successful than those who cannot or will not integrate new migrants into their populations. Policies and strategic communication plans well thought out ahead of time would minimize friction and disruption, and enable the best use of the human capital gained through immigration.

Wherever possible, governments should anticipate where depopulation will occur, and assess that space for future purposes – including potentially as a receiving community for internal or foreign migrants. Think tanks and nonprofit organizations, such as Adaptation Leader, are already proactively developing concepts intended to successfully facilitate movement into receiving communities.

Integration plans will be necessary and must consider:

- Cultural compatibility.
- Resource availability: avoid straining areas with low resources.
- Employment: integrate needed skills into the receiving population.

Agricultural Plans. Governments and agricultural corporations must work together to assure food security. Below are some important factors:

> **Relocation of farms** due to sea level rise, aquifer collapse, extreme temperatures, or other environmental conditions inimical to agriculture. Government must craft policies on land use and repurposing of lands; predict where lands will lose their agricultural value; and create a phased plan for relocating farms to lands where agriculture will still be possible for the foreseeable future.

Diversity: reduce the danger of monoculture crops. Monoculture is a serious threat to our food security today. The industrial scale farming that has become standard over the last 50 years depends on fewer crop species than ever before. This exposes us to an ever-greater risk of human suffering in the event of a crop failure. To reduce the chances of a single pathogen wiping out staple crops and causing severe hardship, agricultural corporations should reduce monoculture, cultivate more heirloom crop varieties, and partner with organizations who are working to preserve, promote, and propagate less-cultivated crop species.

Water: The depletion of both surface water and groundwater will be a major concern for governments to address. Lack of potable water, or lack of access to any water, will be a driving force for internal and international migrations and loss of farmlands and food production capability.

By far the major consumers of water are agriculture and industry, not the individual consumer. Potential solutions that are being explored include more water-efficient agriculture and less water-intensive manufacturing, as well as technologies like desalination, better catchment or distribution systems, and better regulation and water protections.

Energy: Governments and energy corporations must work together to replace fossil fuels with clean-energy sources. There has been progress in this area with the advent of technologies like the electric vehicle. Now, hydrogen-powered cars are beginning to come to market. Solar, wind, hydroelectric, and wave power all are supplying a growing portion of the energy market. However, the transition requires energy for mining, manufacture, transport, installation, and maintenance of these arrays, and much of that energy is still of fossil-fuel origin. But the transition is possible, as Brazil shows us: as of 2023, Brazil generates 93% of its energy from non-fossil-fuel sources, mostly hydroelectric power.

A Global Ark: Preservation of Biodiversity and Accumulated Human Information.

Assuring the survival of the human species requires preserving biodiversity as well as our own accumulated knowledge. Therefore, any effort to bridge the crisis of the next several centuries must include some form or trans-stellar vessel for the maximum achievable preservation of our home-planet's 'Life.' Or, more simply, an Ark.

The idea of an "Ark" to preserve the biodiversity of plant and animal species is not new, nor is the thought that we must preserve our vast and growing trove of valuable information for future generations. But if ever we needed an Ark, the time is now.

Thankfully, the Ark is already under way. It is not a ship, nor a facility, nor an organization; not just one, anyway. It is a movement, a collective but diverse preservation effort.

Many organizations and individuals, professionals, and hobbyists, have seen the need for an Ark. Even if they have not thought of it quite this way, they are already engaged in their own ark-like efforts. There is also already a growing cohort of organizations and individuals who are actively working to preserve species diversity and human knowledge. Since the beginning of the 21st century, as awareness of the problem grows, the response is growing as well.

There is no way that anyone, even governments, corporations, or the extremely wealthy, can achieve the diversity, longevity, or survivability that the Global Ark will need. This makes it essential to promote the idea publicly and encourage anyone with the interest to begin their own efforts to preserve what they can, or build cooperatives to preserve what they can. We also should encourage collaboration among the separate efforts to enhance the effectiveness of the movement.

The most important gifts that we can preserve and transmit to future generations are:

- The genetic diversity of as many plant and animal species and varieties as possible.
- Information *in decipherable* form.

Genetic diversity of plant and animal species.

It is worth repeating here:

> *Adaptation is key to survival.*
> *Diversity is key to adaptation.*

Biodiversity enables the adaptation and continued survival of a wide range of plant and animal species. Because we depend on a healthy biosphere for our own survival and prosperity, it is in our direct interest to preserve as much of this diversity as possible. The dwindling number of familiar food staples to which we now limit ourselves may not be well suited to future conditions; the more biodiversity we successfully retain, the more adaptability we will retain for ourselves as we make necessary shifts to new food crops or new livestock breeds.

Some of the numerous Ark efforts already under way include the famous Svalbard Seed Vault in Norway, which backs up more than 1,700 gene banks around the world. Well-known conservation organizations like the Sierra Club or the World Wildlife Fund are working to preserve natural habitats and animal species. There are also for-profit companies, like Coral Vita, working on less well-known efforts like innovations in coral farming. "Frozen zoos" or "frozen arks" containing tissue samples, stem cells, gametes, and embryos of various animal species are operating in Israel, Germany, the United Kingdom, and elsewhere. There are also individuals achieving significant successes in preserving biodiversity, like Will Bonsall, who collects and shares heirloom seed varieties, or Tom Brown, a hobbyist who has spent his retirement years singlehandedly saving over 1,200 endangered apple varieties.

Information in decipherable form.

Knowledge is power. Therefore, the other main power of the Ark will come from its preservation and transmission of useful information to future generations.

Our ability to use language is one of our greatest survival advantages. For at least 5,000 years, we have had the ability to transmit both concrete and abstract knowledge to future generations by means of the written word. Today, we also have the ability to communicate and to preserve knowledge using video, databases, interactive diagrams, and other complex representations of our knowledge.

Despite the advantages that language confers, we are a short-sighted species too often focused on quick fixes and short-term gains for ourselves, with little grasp of the bigger, long-range, global picture. This is why preserving and transmitting information to future generations is so incredibly important.

Information in all of its forms can play a key role in preserving not only historical or technical knowledge, but human diversity of thought as well. Just as biodiversity enables genetic adaptation, which is key to survival, diversity of thought enables innovations which are key to adaptation and therefore, survival.

Information includes artifacts as well as hard-copy documentation. Museums and archives can and must play a role in the preservation of artifacts and physical documents. Physical documentation is preferable for the preservation of our most important information. Books can last hundreds of years; artifacts, including written scrolls or cuneiform tablets, have lasted thousands of years.

In recent decades, new information increasingly exists only in electronic form, which is notoriously ephemeral and subject to data corruption and loss. It is sobering to imagine how much information we already have lost just due to obsolescence of electronic formats, storage devices, and the machines that read them. The electronic storage of so much information also presents a risk of immense data loss in the event of nuclear electromagnetic pulse or a Carrington-class Coronal Mass Ejection. A loss of that magnitude would create an enormous gap in our documented history and in the useful information available to future generations.

Ideally, to protect against this type of data loss, our most important information should be stored on non-magnetic media. Archives and libraries MUST maintain the tools to read and decipher electronic information, and should be encouraged to develop "hardened" storage facilities to protect magnetic media from disruption.

We also should consider what knowledge is worth saving. Knowledge of science, culture, language, literature, and history have clear value, but much of the "human knowledge" now expanding so rapidly is made up of Internet content like personal blogs or social-media interactions, much of which contains factually incorrect, misleading, or even harmful information. Preserving this type of information could contribute to future anthropological or sociological studies, but it also has the potential to distort facts for future people, just as they distort facts for many of us now.

As to what constitutes our "most important" information, different organizations, governments, or individuals will have varying opinions on this. I would offer two considerations for prioritization.

First, knowledge of the environment and the effects of our activities upon it. As our population falls, we need to continue best practices on environmental conservation. All of the efforts we are now making to curtail climate change come too late to prevent serious environmental changes, but those efforts may yet bear fruit for future generations in the post-peak population era. Fewer people will mean less human-generated impact on the environment, but that must not be regarded as license to return to carelessness or destructive practices.

Second, we must accurately, with neither prejudice nor bias, communicate our shared history and the lessons learned from it, which we are living through now. One of the most important things to recognize is that we are fully capable of recognizing dangerous trends and responding to them, but we historically have ignored them until it was far too late to mount an effective response in our own vital interests.

Despite our human ingenuity that should have enabled us to get ahead of this existential problem, our rising alarm marched in step with climate change only as it actually occurred. The takeaway is that if we hope for the human species to survive into the distant future, subsequent generations must overcome this inertia that results from our short-term thinking and self-interested tendencies. The key to that is clear, accurate information.

There are already active Ark-like efforts under way to preserve information, such as Portico, CLOCKSS, and countless museums, archives, and libraries. These efforts, as well as others engaged with preserving biodiversity, are all supported by people who are well aware of the difficulties involved, and specialize in preservation of the species, information, and objects that we need to maintain our own adaptability as a species. As more people become aware of the need for preservation, new programs, facilities, and projects will arise, adding to the diversity of these efforts and increasing the odds that at least some of them will survive and continue for the long term.

Maximizing the Effectiveness of the Global Ark

Like everything else facing an impending future of instability and resource depletion, all of the current Ark efforts are at some risk of failure or loss. Some physical facilities, forests, animal habitats, or orchards may be threatened by the effects of climate change, or periods of lawlessness or political instability. Some organizations are dependent on donor funding, the continuation of which may be uncertain in the long term. Those sponsored by governments may find themselves written out of the budget in favor of other priorities, or the governments themselves may fail. Efforts steered by private individuals may fail when those individuals pass away. What can be done to mitigate these risks?

First, just as with the diversity of species, the very diversity of existing Ark efforts will increase chances of success. Where one effort may fail, others in different locations, using different methods, or focusing on different priorities may succeed.

If the Global Ark is a movement of diverse preservation efforts, an effort to loosely unify them under an umbrella organization, or at least under a shared rubric, might go a long way toward creating commonly understood mechanisms to foster mutual awareness, collaboration, coordination, and encouragement of new efforts. Uniting the movement in this way could enable the whole to be more effective and more secure than the sum of its parts. Any unification of effort must be well enough defined to enable tangible benefits for participants, but permissive enough to enable the individual efforts to proceed unencumbered by bureaucracy.

The idea of a global "Ark" effort is not new, and thankfully, today we see many separate efforts to preserve plant and animal species, habitat, genomes, and perhaps most importantly for human civilization, information in decipherable form. These efforts have accelerated and multiplied since the turn of the 21st century, and are carried out by a variety of nonprofits, academic institutions, government agencies, and individuals. The best thing we can do for these efforts is support them financially, and support them by either facilitating their efforts, or staying out of their way.

Funding: Getting the Billionaires Involved

We have already noted that the Ark efforts currently under way are helmed by a wide range of entities: governments, nonprofits, academic institutions, a few for-profit companies, and individuals. For practically all of them, funding is the lifeblood of their efforts and will be a perennial concern. Applying for grants or appealing to the public for donations will likely yield diminishing returns over time, and government funding is always subject to cuts related to changing policies or priorities.

This brings me to an observation: at least a few billionaires are worried enough about a coming collapse that they are actively acquiring property and building luxury bunkers in remote parts of the world (see Douglas Rushkoff's work, *Survival of the Richest*). This means that they take the threat of a collapse very seriously, and they have the money to do something about it – at least for themselves.

It would be beneficial to all of us if at least some of these billionaires could be convinced to build, fund, or protect at least some of the efforts to bridge the crisis period, or the Global Ark efforts. To get their participation in a constructive way, they would have to see that at least some select efforts could function in part to support or sustain their own interests. They would need to feel that this would enhance their own control and survivability in the coming collapse. In short, the Global Ark would need to show that at least some of its efforts are aligned with or can support the billionaires' interests.

I am conscious that this thought – co-opting the billionaires – can be criticized as putting at least part of the future of humanity into the hands of the very people who have done much to usher in the coming collapse. The truth is more nuanced: all of us are complicit in degrading the environment, using up resources, and driving climate change just by our sheer numbers. We also are complicit in creating these billionaires by shopping on Amazon, having a Facebook account, buying a Tesla or Starlink service. Billionaires are billionaires because they have figured out how to respond to popular demand. The real issue is *all* of us.

We may benefit by shifting our mindset to a pragmatic approach: we have big global problems that are going to take a lot of money to solve. Billionaires have the resources to achieve what they choose, with better speed and flexibility than governments and probably larger discretionary resources than any other entities on Earth. If billionaires would lend their considerable financial power to these efforts, it would go a long way toward helping to ensure that human civilization will survive the turbulence of the next couple of centuries.

Thinking Very Long Term

Moving to Another Planet

There is another reason to encourage the billionaires to participate in the Global Ark: some of them (and some scientists, like the late Stephen Hawking), believe that mankind needs to colonize other planets within the next century, or face possible extinction. This idea risks expending significant wealth and resources on a space colonization program that will benefit only a few, if anyone at all, and won't do anything to help humanity or other species survive right here on Earth. It is also a patently unfair and elitist idea. Who gets to move to the new colony? Who gets left behind? How much more Earthly environmental cost would there be to launch this interplanetary voyage, to the detriment of those left here?

We evolved here on Earth, for its atmospheric composition, for its plants, animals, fish and microbes, for its gravitational force. We are literally made of the stuff of this planet. If anyone thinks that we can magically find another Earth, with the same atmosphere, the same gravity, the same chemical composition – well, it may be possible, but good luck finding it, getting there, and colonizing it in the next hundred years.

Our immediate goal should not be getting off this planet. Our immediate goal should be cooperating with each other to preserve this planet's biodiversity and the progress that human civilization has achieved so far, enabling ourselves to adapt to current and future environmental changes.

We are quite capable of taking the long view, of cooperative efforts that extend for generations. Consider that those who designed Europe's great cathedrals and laid the foundations knew they would never live to see them completed. Now we must lay the foundations necessary to ensure that humankind's cumulative accomplishments are preserved for future generations.

Closing Points to Remember

- Diversity is the key to adaptability. Adaptability is the key to survival. Therefore, we must maximize efforts to preserve as much diversity as possible to enable maximum adaptability to environmental change in the future.
- Knowledge is power. ACCURATE, DECIPHERABLE information and CLEAR understanding are critical to the control and success of any endeavor. We must maximize efforts to ensure that future generations have access to as much human knowledge as possible, and the critical thinking ability to correctly understand it.
- We have a long history of conflict and competition for resources, and this will continue; but we are capable of cooperation.

Cooperation is absolutely necessary to transmit useful knowledge to future generations.

- Trends and trajectories affecting the human condition, once recognized, can be influenced. We can act, and are already acting, in ways to change human-influenced outcomes for the better.
- The current era of peak human population, from about the mid-19th century to the mid-21st century, represents a highly unusual, artificially produced, and unsustainable human population spike. The next 100-500 years will see readjustment to more sustainable population levels. Wherever fertility is falling by choice, this should be allowed to happen; it is the means to minimizing human suffering and the path to a sustainable future for the human species. The sooner we pass our population peak, the more resources will remain available to us.
- Climate change occurs on a planetary scale over ranges much more extreme than anything we are currently facing. We cannot stop major geological processes or events, but we can use our knowledge to improve our ability to detect them, prepare for them, survive them, and recover from them.

Chapter Three

Navigating the New Paradigm: Stakeholder Capitalism and Governance of Sustainability

Zabihollah (Zabi) Rezaee

Intent of This Chapter

As a practicing accountant, teacher, and researcher, I have witnessed significant changes in business practices, curriculum, and academic research over the past four decades. Initially focused on profit maximization, businesses have shifted towards increasing shareholder wealth and, more recently, creating shared value for all stakeholders.

Sustainability is now an economic and strategic imperative, presenting both opportunities and risks for investors and businesses. Companies are adopting a profit-with-purpose mission, aiming to create shareholder value while meeting social, environmental, and governance (ESG) responsibilities. Globally, businesses are moving from a "shareholder primacy" model, where the board of directors is accountable only to shareholders, to a "stakeholder primacy" model, where the board is responsible for the interests of all stakeholders, including shareholders, creditors, employees, customers, suppliers, society, and the environment. This shift aims to balance wealth maximization for shareholders with welfare maximization for all stakeholders.

Since the turn of the 21st century, this shift has been driven and accelerated by the ongoing challenges of climate change and increasing wealth inequality, which has produced intense social pressures influencing companies to embrace ESG practices. Against the background of this trend, the COVID-19 pandemic came as an abrupt, universal, and completely unexpected exogenous shock to the global economy. The pandemic significantly and suddenly impacted business missions; emphasized the safety, health, and well-being of employees, suppliers, and customers; and affected business operations and corporate governance.

Each of these challenges advanced the shift toward stakeholder primacy, and the stresses of the pandemic offered businesses a unique opportunity to reevaluate and reimagine their corporate governance and sustainability strategies.

With that background in mind, the next portions of this chapter will examine (1) the attributes of shareholder and stakeholder capitalism in promoting business sustainability; (2) the structure of shareholder governance versus stakeholder governance; and (3) the lasting effects of historic crises on the global economy and business sustainability.

Shareholder And Stakeholder Capitalism

Shareholder Primacy and Capitalism

Traditionally, public companies in the United States have operated under the corporate governance model known as the "shareholder primacy and shareholder capitalism" model. This model posits that the primary purpose of a corporation is to generate returns for shareholders; thus, managerial decisions and actions should be focused on creating shareholder value.

The shareholder primacy model has served investors well, by maximizing wealth for them. However, it is criticized for prioritizing short-term profits at the expense of long-term sustainability, performance, innovation, growth, and the corporations' social and environmental impacts. The focus on shareholder wealth creation may not benefit other stakeholders, such as employees, customers, creditors, suppliers, government, society, and the environment. It also has led to wealth inequality and rising populism, prompting questions about the nature and value of capitalism.

Corporations, incorporated under state law, enjoy privileges that allow them to operate, raise public capital, and create wealth for their owners or shareholders; but with these rights come public interests and societal responsibilities. The relationship between corporations and society is complex and evolving, involving various stakeholders such as shareholders, civil society, governments, communities, and consumers. Although corporations contribute to economic growth and prosperity by generating wealth, creating jobs, and benefiting society as a whole, they have a moral and ethical responsibility to consider societal well-being beyond profit maximization.

Policymakers and regulators worldwide are advocating for a more balanced-purpose model for public companies. Despite being separate legal entities with a mission to create value for their owners, corporations can balance their interests with societal well-being by adopting a profit-with-purpose mission. This mission aims to generate desired returns for shareholders while also achieving positive social and environmental impacts.

Stakeholder Primacy and Capitalism

The World Economic Forum recommends that business organizations move from the traditional model of corporate governance/shareholder capitalism to the model of stakeholder governance/stakeholder capitalism.

The stakeholder primacy model holds that public companies should focus on corporate purposes beyond shareholder value. Thus, corporate governance measures and decision-making should also consider every stakeholder who provides capital and contributes to corporate success (including financial, operational, human, societal, and ecological). This would include shareholders, employees, customers, suppliers, communities, society, and the environment.

Under this model, the fiduciary duty of the board of directors is extended to all of these stakeholders. The board should be informed and understand the stakeholder objectives and rationales for focusing on sustainability factors of performance, risk and disclosure, managerial, strategic planning, sustainable operational performance, and executive compensation in promoting long-term corporate value. The board oversees the managerial function of focusing on long-term sustainability performance, and effectively communicates sustainability performance information to all stakeholders.

This emerging concept of profit-with-purpose corporations suggests that public companies have a dual mission: the profit-making function that creates shareholder value, and a social benefit function that protects the interests of other stakeholders, including the environment.

In the past several decades, it appears there has been a move away from pure shareholder primacy and toward stakeholder primacy and related corporate governance measures intended to fundamentally rebalance power among stakeholders. European and Asian companies appear to be moving closer to the concept of stakeholder primacy than their counterparts in North America.

Shareholder Governance vs Stakeholder Governance

Shareholder Governance

The shareholder model of corporate governance is also called the principal-agent theory, because shareholders (principals) provide financial capital to public companies, which then exist for their benefit. The companies are run by management (agents). The principal-agent problem exists because corporations are separate entities from their owners – management needs physical capital (investment funds), and investors need skilled human capital (management) to run the company. The role of corporate governance is to fulfill the primary objective of the company – to maximize shareholder wealth – and to align the interests of management with those of the shareholders.

This supports the agency theory that corporate directors' and executives' fiduciary duties are to shareholders with a residual claim on the company's assets and cash flows. The principal-agent problem arises from two factors: the separation of ownership and control and, most importantly, incomplete contracts or costly enforceable contracts between the agents and principals, known as agency costs.

Business organizations and their investors typically pursue two investment strategies: "impact investing," of "doing good" by engaging in business activities that maximize their benefits to society and the environment; or "socially responsible investing" of "not doing bad" by engaging in business activities that minimize their harms to society and environment. These two investment approaches represent opposite ends of a spectrum ranging from "impact first" to "finance first." The "impact first" strategy emphasizes environmental and social responsibilities of business organizations above and beyond financial returns responsibilities to shareholders. The "finance-first" investment strategy focuses on financial returns as the primary goal of business organizations.

However, corporations should attempt to create a right balance between achieving desired financial returns and obtaining positive and meaningful environmental and social outcomes. The impact investing strategy is gaining global attention as investors are interested in opportunities and risks associated with ESG investments.

Stakeholder Governance

Stakeholder governance recognizes the importance of business survival and continuity in the short term, and sustainable value creation for all shareholders in the long term, as a corporate strategy. This model of corporate governance focuses on the broader view of the company with purpose and profit as the nexus of contracts among all corporate governance participants, with the common goal of creating shared value and maximizing wealth for all stakeholders. These include (1) contractual participants, such as shareholders, creditors, suppliers, customers, and employees; and (2) social constituents, including the local community; society and global partners; local, state, and federal governments; and environmental matters.

Under this view, public companies must be socially responsible – good citizens granted the use of the nation's physical and human capital, managed in the public interest, and sustaining a better environment for the next generations. Public companies' performance is measured based on financial, social, and environmental impacts based on the concept of "doing well by doing good" by creating a right balance between financial returns and positive environmental and social impacts.

Effects of Historic Crises on the Global Economy and Business Sustainability

COVID-19 as a Case Review of a Brief Era & Governance Effects (2019 pandemic -thru- 2024 endemic)

While the modern concept of ESG arose in the first decade of the 21st century, corporate progress in this direction has been inconsistent and varied. In contrast, the 2029-onward COVID-19 pandemic suddenly, forcibly, and substantially affected all aspects of business organizations worldwide, so it warrants our attention.

During the pandemic, traditional functions—such as the board of directors' oversight function, executives' managerial function, and the corporate gatekeepers' monitory function—were significantly curtailed, and their effectiveness was minimized. At the time, it was difficult to predict when and under what conditions these functions might resume in full; thus, this uncertainty created unique challenges for business organizations. The nature of the shock suggested that businesses had no strategic planning or reserved resources to quickly respond to the unfolding crisis and related challenges.

Even after many countries and states in the United States began to reopen their economies, daily activities and business practices were significantly adjusted to a "new normal" in the aftermath of the pandemic, with new office designs, the social distancing of "six feet," remote work, virtual meetings, business continuity, and transformation and changes in corporate governance functions.

The existence and persistence of the 3½ -year COVID-19 pandemic period had lasting impacts on business governance, operational models, business effectiveness, workplace environment, and corporate sustainability. It greatly accelerated the adoption of new measures and practices of corporate governance, including the adoption of new functions, particularly the finance function. Its most noticeable lasting impact was the movement away from shareholder primacy and capitalism toward stakeholder primacy and capitalism. This move created more focus on emerging stakeholder governance and sustainability than on traditional shareholder governance.

The remainder of this chapter examines the new norms and practices of corporate governance structure, including guiding principles, measures, and functions, from the oversight function to the managerial and monitoring functions. Specifically, the traditional corporate governance functions are compared with new norms of corporate governance functions, and suggestions are provided for the proper adoption of changes in corporate governance functions.

A New Paradigm for Corporate Governance

In the aftermath of the pandemic, the new paradigm for corporate governance recognizes the importance of business survival and continuity in the short term, and sustainable value creation in the long term. The new paradigm views corporate governance as coordination and collaboration among all corporate governance participants, from shareholders to boards of directors, executives, and other stakeholders. The goal is to achieve financial Economic Sustainability Performance (ESP) and nonfinancial Environmental, Social, and Governance (ESG) sustainability performance in creating shared value for all stakeholders. It provides a road map for all corporate governance participants, including shareholders, to be attentive in monitoring their investments; for boards of directors in providing effective and engaged oversight; for executives in diligently implementing short, medium, and long-term sustainable business strategies; for and other corporate gatekeepers (auditors, legal counsel, financial analysts) in protecting interests of all stakeholders.

While the emerging new corporate governance paradigm may not resolve all issues and challenges brought on by the COVID-19 pandemic, it enables business organizations to better realize their responsibility for the safety and health of employees, customers, and suppliers, and to redefine their business purpose of achieving financial, social, and environmental impacts.

The three main components of corporate governance structure are: principles, functions, and mechanisms. These three components are very appropriate with the current move toward more effective corporate governance functions using technologies such as virtual board meetings and distance working for executives.

For several reasons, studying the effects of COVID-19 on corporate governance functions is important. First, the idea of remote work and the flexible work schedule has been promoted for some time, and has become a new normal during the COVID-19 pandemic. Second, the use of technology in corporate governance has been developing in recent years, and has accelerated in the post-COVID-19 era (pandemic-down-to-endemic or recurring) by enabling remote work and virtual meetings. Third, future research should address changes in business culture, behavior, policies, and practices in the aftermath of the COVID-19 crisis and their impacts on corporate governance. Finally, despite the devastating effects of this new post-COVID-19 era itself on human lives, economic well-being, and associated challenges, people and business organizations worldwide have demonstrated their resilience and determination to change these challenges into opportunities for improving corporate governance effectiveness and adopting a new paradigm for corporate governance functions.

Theoretically, corporate governance functions serve as mechanisms to reduce information asymmetry between corporations and their owners. Economic shutdowns, home lockdowns and travel restrictions, and social distancing triggered by the pandemic left business organizations with three basic options: (1) suspend all business activities until the pandemic is over;

(2) modify their operations through remote activities; and (3) continue their operations virtually. To survive and maintain sustainability, business organizations were expected to modify their business purpose of protecting the interests of all stakeholders, including investors, customers, suppliers, employees, and communities.

The remainder of this section presents emerging corporate governance principles, functions, and mechanisms, and offers policy, education, research, and practical implications.

Corporate Governance Principles

Corporate governance principles provide guidelines for corporate participants—from the board of directors to executives, auditors, and investors—to collaborate to achieve corporate purpose and mission. Corporate governance principles are emerging and are intended to provide a basic framework and foundation for effective corporate governance that applies to all types and sizes of organizations. Relevant guiding principles of corporate governance are summarized in Exhibit 1.

Exhibit 1: Corporate Governance Principles

Purpose	• Purpose determines why the organization exists, its mission, who the stakeholders are, and its objectives and strategies for achieving the goals. • It creates shared value for all stakeholders, including shareholders, creditors, customers, suppliers, employees, government, society, and the environment. • Every company should have its unique purpose determined in its charter of incorporation to maximize its positive impacts on all stakeholders, and to minimize the negative impacts on multi-stakeholders.
Resilience	• Resilience reflects the corporate ability to cope with undesirable events and maintain its continuity and sustainability. • Resilient corporate governance is sustainable and enduring in that it will easily recover and recuperate from crises. • The corporate resilience in coping with challenges brought on by the COVID-19 era and adjusting operations, procedures, and processes to effectively deal with these challenges is crucial in its continuity as a going concern and its long-term sustainability.

Responsiveness	• The company's timely and appropriate responses to the concerns and challenges caused by the COVID-19 era are important considerations for business organizations and their board of directors and executives. • Proper responses to requests by shareholders and other stakeholders, including investors, customers, employees, auditors, suppliers, and communities, need to be considered and made. • Effective corporate governance is responsive to reasonable requests from all corporate governance participants, emerging issues, and changes in regulations dealing with social distancing remote working environments, among other topics.
Transparency	• Transparency in disclosing favorable and unfavorable financial and non-financial information fairly and clearly to all corporate stakeholders is crucial during and in the aftermath of this continuing post-pandemic COVID-19 *endemic* era. • Transparent communication should be easy to understand for all corporate governance participants. • One important element of well-balanced and fair disclosure is the judgment and decisions made by the board of directors and/or management in response to ongoing challenges and opportunities.

Shared Value	• Shared value creation for all stakeholders can be promoted within the wealth-maximization framework in pursuing the goal of profit-with-purpose for corporations. • Corporations can create the right balance between wealth maximization for shareholders under the shareholder primacy concept while achieving welfare welfare-maximization for all stakeholders (e.g., safety, health, and wellbeing of employees, suppliers, and customers) under the stakeholder primacy concept. • Business organizations must attempt to maximize financial performance and have positive and measurable effects on the environment and society.
Engagement	• Engagement creates incentives to add value and derives performance and results. Stakeholder engagement rebuilds confidence and encourages deliberate, calm, and proper decisions. • Proactive and transparent engagement with all stakeholders in this post-pandemic COVID-19 endemic era is crucial to business continuity and sustainability.

Compliance and Accountability	• Compliance with all applicable laws, rules, regulations, standards, new normal, and best practices in the post-pandemic COVID-19 endemic era is crucial to the survival and sustainability of business organizations. • Accountability reflects the relationship between an organization's objectives, decisions, actions, and performance and develops the cornerstone of corporate governance by continuously monitoring decisions, actions, and performance. • Accountability's main drivers are accepting responsibility, ethical decision-making, and transparency.
Corporate Culture of Integrity and Competency	• A firm's corporate culture of integrity and competency to deal effectively and ethically with challenges brought on by the COVID-19 event plays a key part in setting the standards and enforcing corporate governance. • Corporate culture plays a role of "social control" and the new normal as individuals within the organization and in society are pressured to act a certain way, such as social distancing, remote working, and virtual meetings, among other new normal standards. • Business organizations should express that there will be no tolerance for new normal and standards violations.

Rebuilding Trust	- Business organizations and their board of directors and executives can rebuild trust by providing relevant, reliable, and transparent financial and non-financial information to all stakeholders, particularly those who have been negatively affected by the present COVID-19 endemic era, such as investors, employees, customers, and suppliers. - To rebuild trust, directors must establish proper communication with all stakeholders to understand their concerns, ideas, and feedback in effectively coping with the pandemic. - In collaboration with management, the board of directors should establish strategic plans, policies, and procedures to respond to stakeholders' concerns, issues, and insight to rebuild trust.

Modified Corporate Governance Functions

Corporate governance reflects corporate culture, accountability, and leadership in response to emerging challenges. In response to challenges presented by the COVID-19 crisis, business organizations have recently undergone a series of corporate accountability reforms.

In the aftermath of the COVID-19 pandemic, corporate governance has moved to the central stage of many business organizations, and has transformed from the main focus of protecting shareholders' interests by creating shareholder value, to protecting stakeholders' interests by complying with rules and regulations to maintain business continuity and sustainability.

However, business organizations are experiencing ongoing challenges that affect their corporate governance structure and how they manage their business. There is an increasing interest in corporate governance in the post-COVID-19 pandemic era. Thus, the importance and relevance of corporate governance functions need to be examined in determining the roles, responsibilities, and accountability of all corporate governance gatekeepers, from the board of directors to executives, auditors, regulators, legal counsel, financial analysts, and investors.

In the Exhibit below, we will examine and summarize the seven corporate governance functions: oversight, managerial, compliance, internal audit, legal and financial advisory, external auditing, and monitoring.

Exhibit 2: Corporate Governance Functions

Oversight Function	<ul><li>The fiduciary duties of the board of directors are expected to be extended to multi-stakeholders, including shareholders, creditors, customers, suppliers, employees, government, society, and the environment with the move toward profit-with-purpose mission.</li><li>The board oversight responsibility is extended to good-faith efforts in overseeing the assessment and management of the regulatory and compliance risks as well as overseeing the accuracy, completeness, and transparency of disclosures of risks facing the company.</li><li>In the aftermath of the pandemic, protecting the interests of all stakeholders, from shareholders to employees, customers, and communities, has become a priority of the board of directors.</li></ul>

Managerial Function	- The managerial function of corporate governance is delegated to and assumed by the management team appointed by the board of directors.
- The effective achievement of the managerial function is measured by the alignment of the interests of management with those of stakeholders, including shareholders.
- Management's primary responsibilities are to achieve operational efficiency and effectiveness, comply with all applicable laws, rules, regulations, and standards, properly assess risk, and provide fair and true disclosure of financial and non-financial information.
- Those in the C-suite—including the CEO, Chief Operating Officer, Chief Compliance Office, Chief Human Resources Officer, Chief Legal Office or General Counsel, and Chief Financial Officer—should coordinate efforts and activities to address challenges and risks affecting employees, customers, and the entire organization.

| Compliance Function | - The compliance function of corporate governance creates a regulatory framework for business organizations to effectively operate within and in compliance with the regulatory framework in achieving sustainable performance.
- Regulations should establish a framework within which business organizations can achieve sustainable performance while following COVID-related rules.
- Regulators should provide guidelines to all market participants—from investors to exchanges, public companies, broker-dealers, investment companies, credit rating agencies, public accounting firms, and central clearing parties—to assist them in the proper and effective implementation of business continuity measures, including virtual business and investor meetings and remote work environments. |

Internal Audit Function	- Internal auditors have traditionally performed assurance and consulting services for business organizations in operational efficiency, governance processes, risk management, internal controls, and financial reporting. - Internal auditors are in a unique position to work with the board of directors and management in assessing changes brought on by the COVID-19 era to their organizations, design appropriate policies and processes to address these changes, educate employees about these policies and procedures, and ensure compliance with relevant new normal, standards, policies, and procedures brought on by the COVID-19 era. - The COSO guidance can assist internal auditors in working with management to design and implement strategies and objectives to cope with the challenges of maintaining sustainable performance and business continuity in our post-COVID-19 pandemic (now-endemic) era.

Legal and Financial Advisory Function	- Professional financial advisors perform corporate governance's legal and financial advisory function, the internal and external legal counsel.
- These legal and financial advisors typically assist companies in evaluating business operations' legal and financial consequences.
- In the aftermath of the COVID-19 pandemic itself, legal counsel plays a more important role in ensuring compliance with emerging regulations.
- Financial analysts can provide more effective advice to cope with market volatility caused by the COVID-19 era (both prior pandemic and now recurring endemic CDCP classification).

External Audit Function	- The external audit function of corporate governance is intended to lend more credibility to the published financial statements of business organizations.
- Auditors provide professional opinions on presenting the company's financial statements in conformity with generally accepted accounting principles (GAAP) and the effectiveness of internal control over financial reporting (ICFR).
- External auditors' responsibility has traditionally been protecting investors from receiving misleading and materially misstated financial statements by assuring financial information's accuracy, completeness, and reliability.
- In this present post-COVID-19 endemic era, the role of external auditors as protectors of investors and capital markets has become more relevant and important.

Monitoring Function	• The monitoring function of corporate governance is the primary responsibility of stakeholders, including shareholders. • It can be achieved through stakeholders protecting their interests and the direct engagement of shareholders in looking after their investment. Shareholders play an important role in monitoring public companies to ensure their rights and interests are protected. • Recently, the Business Roundtable (BRT) announced adopting a new Statement on the Purpose of a Corporation to "create value for all stakeholders." • This Statement of Purpose for Corporations is signed by 181 high-powered chief executive officers (CEOs), which recommend the move away from the shareholder primacy concept toward the stakeholder primacy concept that promotes sustainability of creating shared value for all stakeholders.

Corporate Governance Mechanisms/Measures

The corporate governance structure is shaped by internal and external governance mechanisms and policy interventions through regulations. The company's internal and external corporate governance mechanisms have evolved and significantly modified by the post-COVID-19 pandemic era.

Internal mechanisms aim to manage, direct, and monitor corporate activities to create shared value for all stakeholders. Internal governance mechanisms include the board of directors and related board committees (audit, compensation, and nominating committees); a management team led by the CEO, internal controls (operational, financial, and compliance); and the internal audit function.

External governance mechanisms are designed to monitor the company's activities, affairs, and performance to ensure the company and its directors and officers work for the best benefit of all stakeholders. Examples of external mechanisms are laws passed by Congress (Sarbanes-Oxley Act of 2002; CARES Act of 2020) and regulations developed by the SEC, FSB, and IOSCO relevant to public companies, the capital market, the labor market, and the market for corporate control, as well as court decisions, shareholder proposals, and best practices of investor activists.

Recent financial scandals, including the originating COVID-19 crisis, indicate that internal and external mechanisms are needed to protect all stakeholders' interests. The effectiveness and relevance of internal and external corporate governance mechanisms depend on the cost–benefit, efficiency, scalability, and proactiveness.

Corporate governance mechanisms discussed in this section should address these challenges and minimize their negative impacts. Internal mechanisms include a vigilant board of directors overseeing new purpose, mission, objectives, and strategies in the aftermath of the COVID-19 endemic era; executives' determination to implement proper strategies to minimize the negative impacts and ensure continuity of operations; and effective internal controls to achieve the stated objectives. External mechanisms are applicable laws, regulations, rules, and standards intended to reopen the economy and businesses to ensure sustainability and economic and earnings growth in the event of another COVID-19 type shock.

Recent Developments in Business Sustainability and Corporate Governance

In this era of sustainability-oriented investors, directors, and executives, together with the stakeholder primacy mission of business organizations, a major challenge is to show that ESG sustainability factors contribute to bottom-line earnings and long-term return to ensure continuity and earnings growth. The future of corporate reporting will be in the integrated sustainability reports and the related assurance statements by auditors. The next generation of business leaders can play a critical role in promoting and advancing both business sustainability and ESG sustainability.

The efficiency, liquidity, and safety of the financial markets (both debt and capital) have been threatened by the existence and persistence of corporate fraud. These threats have significantly increased uncertainty and volatility in the markets, adversely affecting investor confidence worldwide. Effective corporate governance plays an important role in addressing these crises.

As a practitioner and teacher of auditing and forensic accounting for over 40 years, a scholar who has written many articles on fraud and forensic accounting, and the senior editor of the Journal of Forensic Accounting Research (JFAR), one of the publications of the American Accounting Association (AAA), I understand and emphasize the role of corporate governance in preventing and detecting fraud. Effective corporate governance promotes accountability, improves the reliability and quality of financial information, and strengthens the integrity and efficiency of the capital market, thus improving investor confidence. Poor corporate governance adversely affects the company's potential, performance, financial reports, and accountability, and can pave the way for business failure, inefficiency in capital markets, and loss of investor confidence.

In my book *Financial Statement Fraud*, I discuss how corporate fraud undermines the integrity of financial reports and has contributed to substantial economic losses. As fate would have it, the book was published in March of 2002, just before a wave of corporate accounting scandals at the outset of the 21st century caused the collapse of Enron, WorldCom, and others. The US Congress responded to this wave of corporate fraud by passing the Sarbanes-Oxley Act, which was signed into law on July 30, 2002, to address corporate governance and accountability as well as improving the quality, reliability, integrity, and transparency of financial reports.

In recent years, investors have demanded, regulators have required, and companies have disclosed long-term financial ESP information as well as non-financial ESG sustainability information. Sustainability reporting regulations and standards continue to evolve, and global public companies today face the challenges of adapting proper sustainability strategies and practices to effectively respond to social, ethical, environmental, and governance issues while creating sustainable financial performance and value for their shareholders.

While many business organizations worldwide now present integrated sustainability reports in compliance with the new requirements, some engage in deceptive practices that undermine the integrity of their reporting.

Greenwashing – conveying an inflated impression of the environmental benefits of a company's products or practices – is the most important challenge preventing real progress toward reducing carbon footprint. This problem also damages public trust in corporate sustainability claims of "net zero" emissions.

Double Fraud in Financial Economic Sustainability Performance (ESP) and Nonfinancial Environmental, Social, and Governance (ESG) refers to situations where a company engages in fraud in both ESP and ESG reporting. This can mislead stakeholders into believing the company is more sustainable and financially healthier than it actually is, potentially leading to poor investment decisions and misallocation of resources. Because of these detrimental effects, detecting and preventing double fraud is crucial for: (1) protecting investors from receiving misstated financial and nonfinancial information and ensuring they have accurate information for decision-making; (2) ensuring companies adhere to financial and ESG reporting standards and comply with all applicable laws, rules, regulations and standards that help maintain market integrity and trust; (3) presenting accurate reporting on both financial and ESG metrics to promote genuine sustainable development and corporate responsibility; and (4) helping stakeholders, including investors, regulators, and policymakers, to better evaluate the true performance and sustainability of a company, thereby fostering a more transparent and accountable business environment.

The SEC has recently launched the Climate and ESG Task Force within the Division of Enforcement to develop initiatives to proactively identify ESG-related misconduct consistent with increased investor reliance on climate and ESG-related disclosure and investment. These business leaders and practicing accountants and auditors have an opportunity to drive positive change, promote impact investing strategies, and create a more sustainable and responsible business environment with better financial outcomes and social and environmental impacts. The next generation can contribute to a more sustainable future culture that is environmentally and socially responsible by promoting sustainability as a fundamental value.

Implications for the Future

Modifications in corporate governance structure, including principles, functions, and measures presented in this chapter, can be used by policymakers, regulators, and standard-setting bodies to evaluate the efficiency and effectiveness of new laws, rules, regulations, and standards. Global regulators, including the Securities and Exchange Commission (SEC) and the International Organization of Securities Commissions (IOSCO), have provided regulations and guidelines for business organizations to effectively respond to changes and challenges brought on by any COVID-19-type of future catastrophe.

Regulators should promote ESG sustainability performance disclosure, while public companies prepare integrated sustainability reports with safety, health, and well-being considerations for their employees, customers, and suppliers.

The next generations of business leaders (boards, accountants & auditors, strategic & financial advisors, legal counsels, etc.) should understand the importance of business sustainability with the focus on the achievement of financial economic sustainability in generating the desired rate of returns for shareholders, while attaining nonfinancial ESG sustainability in protecting the interests of all stakeholders including employees, customers, suppliers, communities, society and the environment. The future of corporate reporting will be in integrated sustainability reports and related assurance statements by auditors. The next generation of business leaders can play a critical role in promoting and advancing both business sustainability and ESG sustainability, while showing that ESG sustainability factors more directly contribute to the bottom-line earnings and long-term return to ensure continuity and earnings growth.

To produce the most competent and ethical future business leaders, the next generation of the global academic community expects business colleges and accounting schools worldwide to achieve their mission of providing higher education with a relevant curriculum. Business sustainability and corporate governance education are two areas that are finally receiving long-awaited attention. Business colleges and accounting schools play an important part and an everlasting role in preparing the next generation of business leaders to understand business sustainability and corporate governance, and to use their life-long education and training to act with integrity, upholding the highest level of ethical conduct and the heavy burden of public trust. The future of sustainability education is a dynamic platform that responds to economic, environmental, and social challenges. It will prepare future business leaders who are well-trained and equipped to create a more sustainable and resilient world by addressing these issues.

Conclusion

The shareholder aspect of corporate governance means that shareholders, through their ownership, are entitled to direct and monitor the company's business. They influence governance by electing directors, who appoint management to run the company. Directors and officers, acting as trustees, have primary fiduciary duties to shareholders, though they may also have nonfiduciary duties to other stakeholders with various interests in the company. Shareholders' rights, such as electing directors, proposing actions at annual meetings, and receiving accurate financial information, are legally enforceable. Directors and officers can be held accountable through the courts. However, corporate purpose is evolving, with growing support for stakeholder governance that aims to create shared value and maximize welfare for all stakeholders, not just shareholders.

The initial COVID-19 pandemic caused significant global challenges: a major economic downturn in the U.S., substantial business earnings losses, around 35 million unemployed, disruptions to business practices and supply chains, high employee health risks, and significant stock price volatility.

The present COVID-19 endemic is still our corridor of opportunity for higher transparency. By improving corporate governance, many businesses turned these challenges into opportunities, mitigating negative impacts on all stakeholders and helping the economy and communities recover.

The stakeholder primacy concept, with its profit-with-purpose mission, is expected to continue to gain acceptance among businesses, investors, regulators, and policymakers post-pandemic. Businesses should embrace sustainability, integrating performance, risk, and disclosure factors into their policies and decisions to protect stakeholders, avoid prolonged economic harm, assist those affected, and ensure future earnings growth and economic prosperity.

The important takeaways of this chapter are:

(1) The next generations of business leaders must understand the importance of corporate governance, business sustainability, the continual influence of climate change, and the lasting impact of the original 3½-year COVID-19 pandemic itself.

(2) Businesses worldwide have adopted the concept of profit-with-purpose to create long-term shared value for their stakeholders, from shareholders to customers, employees, suppliers, society, and the environment, and thus the next generations of business and academic leaders should better understand the role of businesses in society.

(3) Business sustainability dimensions of financial, economic sustainability and non-financial environmental, social, and governance (ESG) sustainability performance, and related governance are taking center stage in the global business environment.

(4) There is a move away from shareholder primacy and toward stakeholder primacy as business sustainability factors of performance, risks, and disclosures are demanded by investors, required by regulators, and reported by businesses worldwide.

(5) Business colleges and accounting schools should respond to emerging ESG sustainability initiatives by integrating these important educational topics into their curricula.

(6) The next generation of business leaders should seize the opportunity of promoting positive change and creating a more sustainable and responsible business environment with the goal of achieving profit-with-purpose mission.

(7) The future of sustainability education should be dynamic in training individuals who are equipped with knowledge and ability to effectively deal with emerging environmental, social, and economic challenges.

Chapter Four

Our Quantum Moment in History: Bridging Education Gaps and Introducing the Future of Leadership and Management towards Human Flourishing

Dr. Larry Clay Jr.

When most people think of designers, they think about artists, architects, and artisans. Or they think of tech designers such as UX (User Experience) designers, digital graphic artists, and platform designers. But have you heard of a business model designer? An organization designer? A product designer? Or a design thinker who designs interventions and solutions for problems and challenges we face in our modern time?

If you already know these types of designers exist, then you're probably aware of Herbert Simon, who wrote the seminal essay "*The Sciences of the*

Artificial." It was Simon's perspective that initiated me into this world of design. In his first chapter, he established that what we scientists study and teach in business and organizations is the science of the artificial, contrary to the natural sciences of biology, chemistry, and physics: "Everything man designs is artificial, everything that is already in existence and made by G-d is natural..." (1969: pg7).

Therefore, what we do within the business, entrepreneurship, organizational, computer science, and engineering disciplines is to create artifacts. What we use and redistribute for sustenance and profit are natural resources that can be reconfigured into artifacts or consumed in their natural state. But the designers' mindset and design science can be a benefit.

I am a trained designer and scientist. I also teach entrepreneurship and strategy, and train doctoral students in the business intelligence program. Current research focus and practice encompass designing sustainable systems, including engineered systems, digital systems, business systems, organizational systems, ecosystems, and humans as systems. Most of the is entails experimenting, analyzing trends and patterns, and developing, prototyping, problem-solving, and intervening with solutions for complex systems. I am most interested in how systems are or were designed, how they work interdependently, how they can be improved, and how they can either evolve or be replaced,

One of the greatest design challenges societies are struggling with is a collective effort to mitigate climate change on the global scale. A sustainable planet is a challenge resulting from the interactions between three major complex systems: social systems (human), the ecological system called Earth (natural), and economic systems (artificial). These three systems, along with others that interact with them, constitute a panarchy – a complex set of interdependent systems that can all influence each other.

Reconfiguring this panarchy to repair and restructure what is left of our finite resources, so that future generations can flourish, is the goal of sustainability. However, it has taken half a century to convince people in Western societies that climate change is a real concern of our time. Over the last decade I have been analyzing trends in sustainable development, Corporate Social Responsibility (CSR) programs, and emergent movements such as the B Corp, social innovation, and Conscious Capitalism. Through my observations of the design of the environments, and how humans behave in these environments, I have concluded that our efforts towards sustainability – at least in the US – are fragmented, inefficient, and incremental improvements to deteriorating supply chains, systems, and infrastructure, not to mention the obvious human factors of just being resistant to change.

My present research is focused on sustainable development. This includes staying current with the United Nation's 17 Sustainable Development Goals for 2030[1] (or SDGs, as adopted by Member States in 2015) and constantly tracking the 169 UN indices that underpin these goals. I often ask myself which of these goals would be most useful in designing a strategy that would yield the greatest radical change and impact needed for a sustainable US. I have identified two of these goals – #9 Innovation, Industry & Infrastructure, and #12 Responsible Production & Consumption – that have the best potential to meet the climate change challenge. I came to this conclusion through a design ethnography experiment observing people acting within environments, along with the data to support what can be actively observing in the present: the building blocks of a holistic design.

Designing Intervention within the Paradox of Responsible Production & Consumption

Why are the metrics and index goals underpinning SDG #12: Responsible Production & Consumption so important for the paradigm shift needed to address climate change and achieve this goal? How can US companies produce responsibly and make a profit, and how can we get people to consume responsibly in America?

I do not have an answer or solution - yet. Wicked problems, as described by design theorist Horst Rittel, are difficult to approach and seemingly impossible to solve. Any solution will be complex because the problem is complex, and even then, the best solutions may only minimize or dampen the effects of the problem, but not fully solve it. The nature of the production-consumption problem is just such a wicked problem, with at least one paradox on each side of the system (production vs. consumption).

Let's observe the design of the production side first. The industrial age emerged along with the classical management theories pioneered by Frederick Taylor, Max Weber, Adam Smith, and Henry Fayol. The earlier management models of industry aimed to maximize business profits by maximizing production to serve consumer needs. After the two world wars of the 20th century, industry, business, and economic prosperity (for some) was marked by exponential growth. More products and services emerged during the last 80+ years than any other time in human history. When we include the positive disruptive nature of the automobile revolution, the entertainment revolution, and the technology and digital revolutions, we can reflect on the critical role of innovation in the emergence of new artifacts that seemingly were benefits to the human condition.

But let's reflect on some of the unintended consequences and patterns of behaviors. On the production side of the problem, you have over-production, over-farming, the depletion of natural resources, expressing carbon and other volatile chemicals into the air and water, and tremendous amounts of waste created, then on the consumption side.

On the consumer side, we are overeating, buying artifacts, buying plastics (including single-use plastics), and driving fossil-fuel-powered automobiles just to get out of the house, all of which creates tremendous amounts of waste. Oh, and did I mention that 95% of the innovations created since the mid-20th century, from TVs to TV dinners, are artificial? Yes, and most of these artifacts still exist on this earth as waste in landfills or deep within our ocean floors and coastal banks.

Now let's do a short exercise to examine how most people buy and consume food. We'll use the grocery store as our design framework. First, think about everything you ate yesterday. Was everything natural? Were there any processed, or ultra-processed foods? If you're like many in the US, you probably ate at least one processed food item with artificial ingredients and chemicals listed on the label. Or it might have been fast food for convenience, still processed and full of artificial ingredients.

Next, reflect on your last grocery store visit. Do you notice that most grocery stores have the same general design? If not, the next time you go shopping for food, I challenge you to notice where the "natural" food items like proteins, , dairy, vegetables, and fruits are located; then notice where all the processed, "snack," and artificial foods are located. Observe their location, labeling, branding, and pricing!

Some of you already know that the majority of your own food choices are in the "less than natural" and "blatantly artificial with minimum nutritional value" food aisles. This is at least partly because the corporate interior designers designed the layout of the grocery store by first understanding the human condition and needs. Then marketing and sales designers structured a merchandising shelving system, so non-perishable and "slow" perishable items can be packaged and marketed heavily to create a perception as being affordable, nutritionally filling, and satisfying to consumers. It can be eye-opening to notice how this affects our food choices. You get more food but with less nutritional value.

What I hope you have recognized with this exercise is that some of your choices and decisions are heavily dependent on self, while other decisions are influenced by designers.

To approach the production side of this problem will take more than just having a CSR program or running greenwashing PR campaigns. It will require sustainability-focused innovation with intelligently designed supply chains to distribute appropriate and sufficient goods for consumption. The classical management models of overproduction, excuses of externalities, profit maximization, and influencing societal overabundance and wastefulness are not good fits for the global environment, nor is it appropriate and sustainable for the today's digital era.

I believe the greatest change mechanism available to us humans is the opportunity and determination to change thyself. Fixing the consumption side of the problem collectively requires each of us to act individually. I've been susceptible to the routines of making poor food choices and consuming processed foods for taste, comfort, and price over basic nutritional value. I have fond memories of going to the local grocery store with my grandmother on Saturday mornings. I would push the basket, my sister managed the coupons, and as a treat at the check-out stand, I would always be rewarded with a bag of Flaming Hot Cheetos – my personal food addiction!

To be honest, I was probably well into my 30s before I weaned myself from my personal tradition of eating those Flaming Hot Cheetos. What was instrumental in catalyzing this change for me was learning and adopting the practice of conscious attunement, also known as mindfulness practices. It wasn't until then that I understood how biofeedback played a critical role in how I operated, thought, made decisions, and socialized within my environments. The more I made decisions to consume less natural, less than nutritious, artificial food items, the more my body and mind reacted within my natural human feedback loops to manifest into the world poor decisions, maladaptive relationships with other people, disregard of the natural environment, tremendous weight gain, and exacerbated mental illness. When I made the conscious decision to incorporate more natural, living foods into my eating habits, and give up my consumption vices, my body and mind manifested a transformed version of me with weight loss, better eating habits, better relationships with myself and others, and a sense of flourishing vitality overall. Later in this chapter, I'll share more about my personal quantum (conscious) journey and offer some practical tools you can use to practice intentional change models for personal development.

Designing the Future of Innovation, Industry & Infrastructure

Now, let's unwrap the second SDG goal that will potentially offer the greatest opportunity for eco-systematic change. The goals of SDG #9: Innovation, Industry, and Infrastructure aim to build resilient infrastructure, promote inclusive and sustainable industrialization, and build a support system with an evolutionary fitness for the fostering of innovation. The primary objective is to encourage sustainable economic growth, create jobs, improve living standards towards individual flourishing and well-being, and to ensure that the technological advancements of artifacts and infrastructure developments are environmentally friendly (reducing or eliminating harm) and benefit most segments within a society.

It is well documented and agreed upon within scholarship communities that the one catalyst that ensures evolutionary fitness or flourishing vitality within an economic system is value creation – the continuous designing of artifacts through entrepreneurship and the creation of organizations, business ventures, and workforce development. It is necessary to establish a pipeline for the emergence of new technology, firms, organizations, and what it means to work for economic and financial gains as humans. Without the consistent emergence of new technology and organizations, there would be no replacement for existing firms within ecosystems to maintain the generativity of transactions and flow of currency. This is important in two major areas: lifecycle of the firm, and the emergence of valuable innovation. Let's look at these two topics.

First, consider the average lifecycle of a business. Over the last 100 years, we've seen that the resilience and vitality of many firms has diminished. Firms are closing, shutting down, or getting acquired at a much more rapid pace than in the past. If you reflect on the last 60-plus years and think about the Fortune 500, you will notice that the list of top performing firms continually changes. A study on the volatile nature of the Fortune 500 revealed that in each decade, the turnover rate of listed companies increased over time, projecting the rapid growth of new firms, sectors, and industries mostly driven by technology, energy, and financial services. For example, firms on the Fortune 500 list during the 1960s - 1970s averaged a lifecycle of 30 years prior dropping off the list. Fast forward to the millennium, and the findings show that firms spend an average of ~10 years on the Fortune 500 before the firm dissolves, fails, or gets acquired and ultimately removed from the list. This trend shows that a firm's existence and ability to sustain and maintain its organizational system is becoming shorter.

For firms to maintain longer lifecycles and develop evolutionary fitness, there is a critical need to foster and rapidly increase more sustainable innovation and value creation. We also can anticipate that existing large firms will inevitably need replacements within ~10-year timeframes to ensure the overall fitness of the economic system. Without functional entrepreneurship within the economic system, the economic system will dampen, with a reduction of transaction opportunities to promote the generative and appreciative nature of currency and goods interactions.

Another concern is innovation. Innovation in general is necessary, but is not enough to maintain the economic system. We specifically need more sustainable innovation intentionally designed for human flourishing and well-being, and fewer "innovations of distraction," which are the artifacts and attractors that detach us from the nature of being human.

Let me provide a few examples of "innovations of distraction" and couple the innovations with the generations they influenced in their time. Think about the Baby Boomers, the consumption of radio, and the rise of consumerism; or my generation, Gen X, and our relationship with television and cable, video games, and the rise of fast food; or the Millennial generation, and how they consume social media, digital platforms, the internet, and virtual and augmented reality. This gives you a better idea of what is meant by "innovations of distraction. " Studies have revealed that these innovations have properties of overconsumption embedded within their design, and they have been proven to shift our mindsets and influence behaviors away from human tasks such as exercising, healthy eating, personal development, and healthy consumption of digital and visual entertainment, to name just a few.

We've lived in this reality of navigating, exchanging, using, and consuming both natural and artificial resources; however, my greatest concern is the potential of more people gravitating towards a value preference of artificiality and moving further away from connecting to the natural processes and state of the universe and human values in exchange. the late Wm. Van Dusen Wishard said it best in his August 11, 1982 essay to D.V. Poole, *Understanding Our Moment in* History:

> "Thus, we need to understand technology at a deeper level, and be aware of how it has changed people and entire societies throughout history. Technology is not simply a passive tool. It changes us as we use it; it alters our perception of life. The automobile changed the basic structure and relationships in the American family. TV changed the content and nature of politics. The Internet is diminishing our sense of time and

place and shredding traditional cultural and information structures."

Here, Wishard frames the relationship of technology artifacts and their influences on everything from altering our perceptions of life to amplifying a culture of addiction with our smart devices. As I reflect on His essay, I find some similarities with my overall written chapter in thought, position, and inquiry. The profound statement he made on this topic of innovation, sustainability, and the human experience was, "…we must not just use technology; but study it and how it is affecting our culture and mindsets.". What Van Wishard wrote about and described in his essay of over one-and-a-half two decades ago, I am actively practicing and writing about as a design scientist in the present.

Now that I've offered a framework for understanding design, and a strategic framework for approaching the production-consumption challenge and fostering sustainable-focused innovation and infrastructure, I would like to share one of the most compelling inquiries on the innovative process that keeps me up at night. If innovation is the key to maintaining the economic system and has been proven to be the greatest opportunity for economic development and prosperity of a free society, then why doesn't the US have entrepreneurship curriculums in secondary and middle schools? Why did it take me four failed ventures, an MBA, and a PhD to get the necessary access to entrepreneurship education and the practical tools needed for designing business ventures? How can theories and frameworks from modern quantum science and consciousness help designers and entrepreneurs approach leadership, business venturing, and product development with the impact needed to shift organizations, communities, and societies towards full spectrum flourishing?

I've started preliminary research on the first inquiry, and have confirmed that access to education in entrepreneurship, as well as business, is isolated in higher learning centers. There is evidence of a handful of private schools with business curriculum offered, and in some public schools across the nation, economics is offered. There were also non-profit organizations identified, mostly in highly populated urban settings, that offered entrepreneurship workshops, bootcamps, and other support services for high school age and young adults interested in entrepreneurship. But of course, they operated with deficits and finite resources.

The Global Trends toward Sustainable-Focused Innovation

I would be remiss if only providing context on the US and Western perspectives of production-consumption balancing in economic systems and the importance of innovation to maintain the economic ecosystems. It is well established in geopolitical scholarship and think tank circles that China is on a trajectory of changing the distribution of geopolitical power, and the rise of Asia is becoming the dominant geopolitical reality. The modernization of Chinese city infrastructure has lifted over 400 million of its people out of absolute poverty, and that's more people than there are citizens in the US! Another trend that we see in China, India, and parts of the Middle East is an increase of STEM PhDs; and it was estimated years ago that the continent of Asia would soon have 90% of all STEM related PhDs living there.

Wishard also highlighted in his essay, "Goldman Sachs estimates that by 2040 the four largest economies in the world will be China, the U.S., India and Japan – in that order." What Wishard and Goldman-Sachs suggest is that within my lifetime, I will possibly experience a future where the US will no longer be the dominant world power as we have been for most of the last century. Although it seems daunting as an American, and a hard pill to swallow, I sense that this is a part of the evolution of the global order.

Future scenarios of cyber warfare, social dysfunction and conflict, misinformation campaigns, political polarization within and between states, resource depletion, and severe losses can be understood as consequences of climate change. A concurrent observation is our inability to change as a collective. And, yes, over the last decade I have been sensing the emergence of what has become known as "a time of polycrises." Our future may unfold either on a transformational journey towards flourishing and well-being of people and planet, or facing the task of reconstructing the next social order post-bellum. Regardless, I will offer two sets of tools that will be useful for either future scenario.

One tool is *design thinking*, which will be useful to enhance community stakeholders' intelligence and skillsets complemented with modern STEM education for professional development. When learned, stakeholders will gain an understanding of how to employ design science to everything from designing systems, infrastructure, and organization to designing the self for flourishing. This is also consistent with the direction of findings of the systems of governance scholar, Dr. Zabihollah Rezaee.

The other set of tools I offer is what quantum theorist Danah Zohar calls *quantum thinking*. Adopting practices of interconnectedness to strengthen human capabilities for personal, professional, and spiritual development is a key feature of quantum thinking and is a part of the process of managing the quantum self. I will explain both tools and their relevance to emergent theories of quantum management.

Design Thinking and STEM education for Professional Development

Design thinking is a human-centered approach to problem-solving that emphasizes empathy, creativity, and rationality. It involves understanding the needs and experiences of people, defining problems from their perspectives, ideating potential solutions, prototyping, and testing those solutions iteratively.

This methodology is particularly relevant in reorganizing and restructuring infrastructure and industry in a post-bellum environment, where communities are often dealing with the aftermath of conflict and the need for renewal. By focusing on the lived experiences of individuals and communities, design thinking can help identify critical needs and innovate solutions that are both practical and impactful, promoting cooperation and collaboration.

At the center of adapting to a design thinking mindset is design cognition development. Design cognition development is an essential aspect of the design process in any venture, as it involves cultivating the skills and mindset necessary for creative problem-solving. This development encompasses the ability to frame and reframe problems, generate multiple solutions, and synthesize complex information. In a post-bellum context, design cognition allows practitioners to navigate uncertainty and ambiguity, while fostering resilience and adaptability to the greater environment. For example, when rebuilding a community's infrastructure, designers and stakeholders must consider various factors such as cultural context, resource availability, complexity, and long-term sustainability, all of which require advanced cognitive skills.

Absent the post-bellum context, the future state is just a continuum of the present, with economies and people thinking and conducting "business as usual." In either future scenario, the need is still the same. Our "doing and thinking-as-usual" models are failing both business and political leadership in these new times, and leaders and scholars around the globe, are advocating for new ways of thinking with new leadership and management practices that are so radical that they reconfigure the systems we have taken for granted and change inside out and upside down. Leadership experts suggest that transformative thinking and doing, rather than classic linear thinking, has the greatest potential of implementing the radical change needed for the next paradigm shift in the Digital Era.

Design science complements education in STEM (Science, Technology, Engineering, and Mathematics) as well as within the management disciplines. This convergence provides a structured yet creative framework for tackling complex problems and designing artifacts and organizations. Design science integrates scientific methods with creative processes, enabling practitioners to systematically explore solutions while considering human factors. Integrating design science with STEM can lead to innovative engineering solutions that are not only technically sound but also socially and culturally relevant, keeping humans and natural resources central to the approach. Management education, on the other hand, benefits from design science by incorporating design thinking principles into strategic decision-making, leadership, entrepreneurship and venturing, and organizational and personal development.

Whether we will transform the existing community or need to rebuild the community post-bellum, I offer design practitioners some simple best practices in Design Thinking to establish the new community:

- **Empathy and Community Engagement:** Prioritize understanding the needs, desires, and challenges of the affected community through active listening and engagement.
- **Collaborative Problem-Solving:** Foster collaboration among multidisciplinary teams, including local stakeholders, to co-create solutions that are inclusive and sustainable. Maximize efforts utilizing diversity as a competitive advantage.
- **Complex Systems:** Develop competencies to understand complexity and complex adaptive systems. Many societal problems are complex, yet we often approach them with linear solutions in problem-solving. Create a learning environment to promote complex thinking over linear thinking.
- **Prototyping and Iteration:** Embrace a mindset of experimentation by prototyping solutions through simulations and failing

fast, and iterating based on feedback, ensuring continuous improvement to whatever is being designed.
- **Cultural Sensitivity:** Respect and integrate cultural values and traditions into the design process, acknowledging the community's unique identity and heritage while taking advantage of diversity.
- **Sustainable Practice:** Focus on long-term sustainability by considering environmental impacts and resource efficiency in all design decisions.

By following these simple best practices, leaders, design practitioners, and community stakeholders can contribute to the holistic and resilient reconstruction of communities, ensuring that infrastructure and industry are not only rebuilt, but also reimagined in ways that foster growth, well-being, and harmony that contribute to flourishing communities.

Quantum Thinking: A Practice of Interconnectedness to Strengthen Direct Intuitive Capabilities for Personal, Professional, and Spiritual Development

> *"When you increase connectivity, new intelligence emerges…a quantum leap in consciousness."* —Complexity theorist Ralph Abraham

I'm pretty sure most of you have heard the saying, "… if we want to change and improve the conditions of the world, then we must change ourselves first." I'll take it a step farther and agree with how quantum scientists David Bohm and others have framed it: "If we are really going to create a better, wiser, and more sustainable world, then we will need to *think* differently, and to *organize* differently." Both statements point to the same observation and intervention, i.e., to change our mindsets, individually and collectively.

Why do we need such change? In the Western world, we have experienced ourselves, our organizations, and our societies as being composed of atomistic bits, pieces of a whole that are separate from the greater environment, Nature. We treat the natural environment as a resource to be utilized, separate from the individual self. Historically, there have been positive outcomes that have emerged from this separateness mindset. It was instrumental in developing business, innovation, economic prosperity through industry, social institutions, and advancements in technology; but with piecemeal, fragmented approaches, the outcomes were not holistically shared amongst and within the whole of various societies and nation-states. If there were any lesson to learn from the COVID-19 pandemic, it is that we must attune, learn, and adapt to the greater environment and develop a holistic relationship and mindset to better understand ourselves, our planet, and our human actions comprehensively as one.

Our current management paradigms are not as useful as they once were and are not equipped to handle the challenges we face in the realities of the Digital Age. In our traditional models of management and leadership, we do not have the capability to control the greater environment with left brain creativity and right brain logic. In contrast, an emerging framework and model of management and leadership called quantum management is a tool and solution to catalyze the new management paradigm needed to respond to the emerging wicked problems of 21st century realities.

Quantum Management is rooted in the new paradigm bequeathed to us by research in consciousness, quantum physics, and its younger sibling, complexity science. It is difficult to unwrap quantum physics in a chapter. Quantum management isn't just another theory of management. It is a new paradigm, or new way of thinking and doing, for leaders, those that are assigned functional roles in management, and everybody else – the conscious whole. I would recommend the book *Zero Distance* by Donah Zohar, who has done an outstanding job of outlining the key constructs that best highlight the differences between the classical paradigm of business and organization (Newtonian-Taylorian principles) vs. the quantum paradigm of business and organization. I will briefly summarize and reference her work.

Newtonian physics theorizes that the world, science, and reality for that matter, is mechanistic, atomistic, and deterministic. What's available in the universe is either a particle or a wave which reacts to forces, and is isolated and separate as a piece of a whole; and this knowledge is absolute. Zohar correlated these fundamental principles of Newton's physics theory with Fredrick Taylor's fundamental management theory structuring how companies and leaders operate under Taylorian-Newtonian management models. The classic industrial company under Taylorism operates like a machine; structured hierarchically in siloed functional compartments, bureaucratic, rule-bound, particle-like, with a division of labor. People in companies usually agree to one best way of execution with the most simplistic point of view. Companies are usually reactive, not proactive to the environment, and the company is perceived as isolated and separate from the environment. Leadership in such companies treated themselves as "we know best" and "no one lower in the hierarchy can question us," implying to the employees that the leaders had absolute power, control, and authority.

Although I believe there are many companies, communities, and nation-states with leaders that still operate with this mindset, there has been incremental progression in leadership techniques, hierarchical organizational systems, and governance structures that aren't as rigid and controlling as organizations and leaders were 150_+ years ago. But there is still tremendous opportunity to change.

Now let's briefly unwrap some of the key principles and features of quantum physics and relate it to elements of what Zohar coins the Quantum Company. I recommend Maturana's essay, "*A special edition devoted to autopoiesis,*" which provides the framework to understand the difference between complex adaptive systems (CADs) and mechanistic systems. He defined CADs as having properties of "living" systems, or autopoietic and defined mechanical systems as having properties of "built" systems, or allopoietic. A few features that distinguish autopoietic from allopoietic is that living systems are self-organizing, autonomous, difficult to control, and have self-production capabilities, features which, at present, no machine or designed mechanical system, including AI, has.

Complex adaptive systems are properties of quantum physics as mechanical systems are properties of classic physics. A few other differences between classical and quantum physics are that in the quantum realm, particles and waves aren't separate but integrated as one, or BOTH. It is helpful to understand the principle of *superposition*, which is the ability of a quantum system to be in multiple states at the same time until it is measured (e.g., is it 0 or 1, or 0 and 1, or neither 0 nor 1). The principles of quantum entanglement, multiple potentialities, and interconnectedness posit that on a subatomic level, everything is connected to everything else. Two sub-atomic particles in any space and time will connect, leave a mark on the other, and travel billions of light years away, but despite physical distance and separation, changes induced in one will affect the other.

The last principle of quantum physics I will share is my favorite, and it is Heisenberg's Uncertainty Principle. The quantum reality itself is indeterminate and cannot be controlled. Thus, Heisenberg's Uncertainty Principle suggests that we must always content ourselves with partial truth and ambiguity when trying to know the whole. At best, we can humble ourselves and ask questions to uncover deeper unknown truths. Inquiry creates answers, and the lesson leaders can take away from Heisenberg's Uncertainty Principle is that our inquiries affect the answers we get. If we inquire differently, different answers emerge.

Remember, it is more than "inquiry in exchange" with other humans, or even our own analytical and creative brains that ponder questions. Scientists like me, in quantum management and leadership, are finding empirical evidence of a neurological feedback mechanism, where there are sections of the human brain that exchange signals from what Zohar calls "...a participatory universe in which our questions, our projects, our experiments, our decisions, even our character, [shape] the world we live in".

We theorize this to be the process of direct intuitiveness that initiates and informs intuition, and more specifically, spiritual intuition. Consider Frances Vaughn's observation: *"Spiritual intuition can be perceived as a holistic perception of reality [that] transcends rational, dualistic ways of knowing and gives us - the perceived individual - a direct transpersonal experience of the underlying oneness of life."*[2]

Spiritual intuition can be perceived as 'a holistic perception of reality [that] transcends rational, dualistic ways of knowing and gives us - the perceived individual - a direct transpersonal experience of the underlying oneness of life. Spiritual practitioner Chogyam Trungpa says, "...the practice of meditation prepares the mind for spiritual intuition by clearing away obstacles which ordinarily impede access... but as this kind of [intuitive] intelligence becomes more active and penetrating, the vagueness begins to be pushed aside and dissolves."

So far, our findings are showing that leaders, designers, entrepreneurs, figures of politics and faith, and people in general who practice conscious living all share a common routine of taking time to connect and attune to the universe; and the majority of them have shared profound experiences that have transformed their lives in making better decisions, being more mindful and aware of actions, and worrying less about things.

Let's apply these same principles to structure what we mean by the term "Quantum Company." A Quantum Company is a complex adaptive system, but conceptually, a conscious living system that self-organizes (with people), has many parts to a conscious whole, has many points of view, and is designed with agility and adaptiveness for resilience and evolutionary fitness. Quantum companies stay attuned, connected, and in constant dialogue with actors within the greater business ecosystem, including their customers, suppliers, partners, employees, and other stakeholders. Quantum companies encourage inquiry at all levels, internal and external to the organization; and they encourage the idea of their internal actors "co-creating amongst partners," instead of "employees working together in silos."

My hope is that this chapter further piques your curiosity to learn more about Quantum management and design science. And that you will want to learn more about how adopting these tools, competencies, and practices will be instrumental in organizations and our societies in response to the ever-changing, evolutionary system called the Quantum reality, which is the ultimate control of the Quantum order – the Universe.

By the end of year 2025, my next book, My Soaring: The Quantum Designer, should be released. It will be a set of stories reflecting on entrepreneurs, designers, and business venturers and their pursuits of value creation to problem-solving and how adopting Design thinking and Quantum thinking played a role in our successful ventures. In this chapter I was only able to touch the surface in framing the challenges of achieving sustainable futures, sharing that our efforts aren't working with our current management models, and offering two promising management tools that will provide us with better approaches and models to address the emerging challenges of now and evolving futures. In closing, if you don't remember anything else about this chapter, remember this:

- Reframing education through the lens of design has the potential to have better learning outcomes that converge the natural (biology, chemistry, physics) and the artificial sciences (management, business) to build a better future for humanity.

- Developing spiritual intuition is a human competitive advantage when consciousness is amplified through practices of interconnection. Strengthening your intuition will guide your thoughts in the Quantum reality that will reflect how "we" operate in the world – optimistically towards more conscious cooperation with healthy competition.

Chapter Five

What Does a Solutions Engineer Do with Electronic Reporting Platforms in Smaller and Mid-Size Firms?

Dennis J. Easter

Growing up, I was surrounded by people who made things. I was always attracted to those who could design, build, and produce. As I moved through college and then my first set of operational jobs, I focused (and eventually became considered an authority) on "solutions engineering."

What is solutions engineering? Each week, my firm and I sit with large and small firms and ask: What value can we add and how can we improve the organization's value to society and the market through technology platforms and process improvement? Solutions engineering is about taking complex sets of existing assets and making them more efficient, more productive, and then accounting for themselves for further improvements.

This is not the same as generating the big data that runs the world's banks. Instead, it is about the information platforms that run manufacturing operations. In my career, this has gone from a remote, on-the-factory-floor specialty to a major new global problem-solving trend. From Siemens and Toyota, to giants even bigger like Exxon and Shell and Unilever—all these giants now have dozens if not hundreds of solutions engineers working across vast territories.

How do they do this? And how can we share that knowledge of complex global multinationals with an ordinary firm of several hundred staff?

I have worked most of the last 30 years helping businesses be better. Most of my energies are spent helping small and medium size manufacturers become more efficient, profitable, and competitive. 83.4% of the approximately 600,000 manufacturing companies, according to the 2021 study, employ less than 1,000 employees. These small businesses are important contributors to their local economies around the country. They provide a strong economic multiplier because of their spending patterns and cost structure.

Considering recent history, one can also see the importance of a domestic manufacturing base. The supply chain disruptions from COVID, shipping port and waterway disruptions as well as ongoing geopolitical tensions, exposed the risks associated with a globally distributed supply chain. My goal is to help make "Made in the USA" the primary label again on as many products as possible.

In learning how to do my work more effectively, I have studied labor relations, regulations, transportation, and production processes. In short, I have learned how to put all this learning into a lattice of decision-making models. I think we can re-establish a vibrant manufacturing base, but it will take something America has struggled with: cooperation, even with people we disagree with.

I believe a strong domestic supply chain and manufacturing base is key to economic stability and environmental sustainability. To prepare for the future with a strong domestic supply chain, I offer the knowledge and advice in this chapter for your consideration.

Constants in the Smaller Organizations

In my thirty years as a working practitioner, I have worked with companies from coast to coast. The small- and medium-size firms have limited resources, so they must be run by smart people, owners that care for the employees and feel a great responsibility as the leader of a family.

Because of scale, small problems in these businesses have a much greater impact. Since the owner, in most cases, is directly involved in the day-to-day operations, the owners are focused on making the next payroll, finding the way to grow sales so the business can survive, and always looking for ways to create some breathing room.

Over the last thirty years I have seen small businesses consistently have to manage, struggle with, and innovate to solve the following constant issues:

- The balance in labor relations
- Successfully adopting technology
- Managing distributed supply chains
- Avoiding hubris in decision making
- Small business growth to a plateau
- The failure of formal education
- The importance of a wide variety of relationships
- The fact that large companies tend to be poor partners with small business

Consider these in context of your own experience. When you consider the "ideal" or even the "better," where do you and your organization fit? Take a moment to evaluate your current state in each of these areas. What is going right? What can happen to make things completely fail?

As mentioned earlier, I want to see products currently made offshore produced in the U.S. To that end, the section on extended supply chains is much longer than the others. It is also one of the more complex topics I have studied.

Analysis of Distributed Supply Chains

Distributed supply chains are a relatively new concept. In the last century they grew in prominence, often growing out of the need for cost reduction of the increased supplier capacity. The local blacksmith could no longer keep pace with demand, which led to buying the metal assembly from a foundry several states away. Then as industrial capabilities in developing nations came online and they were able to produce mass quantities at lower prices, they replaced the foundries a few states away as primary suppliers, primarily as a cost-cutting measure.

Let's examine a number of important aspects of distributed supply chains.

Systems Theory

Supply chains are systems made up of multiple members, linked to produce a result. If you consider supply chains in the context of systems theory, a global supply chain may offer advantages such as cost efficiency, access to diverse markets, and specialization. It also comes with inherent risks. Some key risks associated with a global supply chain:

Risk	Consideration
Interconnectedness	Because they involve multiple suppliers, manufacturers, and distributors across different regions, disruptions in one part of the world can quickly cascade through the entire system. (Remember COVID.)
Vulnerability to Disruptions	This vulnerability corresponds to the system's sensitivity to external forces that test a system's resilience and adaptability in the face of disturbances. The series of events since 2020 demonstrate this vulnerability.
Information Asymmetry	Lack of accurate and timely information across the supply chain can lead to misjudgments, inefficiencies, and increased response times in addressing issues.
Quality Control Challenges	Ensuring consistent product or service quality becomes challenging when dealing with multiple suppliers and manufacturing processes worldwide.

Additionally, aside from systems theory and focusing on sustainability of global supply chains, global supply chains often introduce practices that are unacceptable in certain domestic markets and would affect a company's reputation through multiple bottom-line reporting.

Environmental

Much emphasis is given to reducing carbon emissions in the United States and other developed economies. However, developing economies as well as China are not held to maintain these same standards for environmental impact such as carbon emissions, chemical discharge into natural waterways, toxic chemical dumping and improper disposal of waste generated, or deforestation. Much of this is due to the lack of government oversight. While these certainly cause long-term damage, it provides suppliers in these countries with a competitive advantage through lower production costs.

Social

Long-term success, which leads to long-term value building, depends on being a good citizen. The narrative of extended supply chains is replete with stories of sweatshops, child labor, forced labor. In the context of social responsibility, a company using an extended supply chain needs to be aware of the risk and expend the resources to monitor and manage this. Additionally, the safety and employee health requirements placed upon foreign producers are more relaxed and often lead to employee accidents and injuries, which in turn may expose the company sponsoring the work to legal liability and reputation risk.

Governance

Adding foreign operations to an enterprise adds complexity to corporate governance. Each jurisdiction adds another layer of factors to the decision-making process. Factors include more regulations to comply with, taxation, cultural differences, and the potential corruption that can put operations and projects in jeopardy unless participating in illicit payoffs. Creating a consistent governance policy in light of the various operating environments presents unique challenges and increases the true cost of doing business in foreign countries.

Ethical and Regulatory Risks

Varied ethical standards and regulatory frameworks in different countries can expose the supply chain to legal and reputational risks as well. The external environment influencing the system is not affected by the system. Rather, the system is required to navigate through different legal and ethical landscapes. Unethical practices such as corruption, bribery, or fraud may be commonly accepted practices in other regions, but when considering business sustainability and citizenship, they must be addressed.

Foreign Supplier Compliance – Chain Transparency

More and more often, companies are being held accountable for the activities of their upstream supply chain. The OECD (Organization for Economic Cooperation and Development), the forum where governments from countries with market-based economies formulate policies to promote sustainable economic growth, has supply-chain transparency as one of its major tenets, including holding downstream companies accountable for actions of their upstream suppliers. Areas for monitoring include fair labor, environmental impact, corruption, and human rights.

As previously mentioned, the more distributed areas to be monitored, the more difficult to monitor and ensure compliance. Starting with due diligence, companies need to confirm compliance from their upstream suppliers. All of the extra effort required to create supply-chain transparency and limit chain liability all add to the cost of the goods produced in the supply chain and need to be considered.

Total Cost of Ownership

Finally, often the decision to use a foreign supplier is based on the product purchase cost. However, a deeper dive into many instances will reveal that the total cost of acquisition is much different. While the price on the purchase order may be cheaper, there are additional costs that need to be considered. Many times, orders from foreign suppliers are much larger than the immediate demand plan.

I know of one company that purchased seven years of stock for a particular item to meet minimums for the foreign supplier. First, imagine having seven years of inventory for an item on the balance sheet instead of a portion of that in cash. Second, the inventory-carry costs need to be considered. Warehouse space isn't free, and if you are in a constrained space, you may have opportunity costs for stocking higher levels resulting from importing. When considering foreign suppliers, account for all costs, not just the PO cost and freight.

Considerations for Future Success

In the current environment of increased geopolitical turmoil, developing a domestic supply chain will be key to mitigating the risk that global turmoil creates. However, know that the other areas previously discussed will be required to adapt to the change.

Additionally, larger public companies at the end of the supply chain need to consider the supply chain in the entirely of ESG management. Certainly, climate change is the headline leader when it comes to ESG. However, given the differences between the US and other economies—in environmental regulations for everything from energy generation to toxic waste disposal—companies need to consider the entirety of the supply chain, not just the immediate economic cost. When considering the supply chain in ESG, consider the child labor, human rights practices, and social progress in contrast to domestic suppliers.

Secure the Supply Chain

As previously discussed, developing a consolidated domestic supply chain provides an opportunity to gain a competitive advantage by mitigating the risks of an extended supply chain. When we look to the future, indications are that geopolitical tensions will only increase. Black Swan events will become more common. The outside factors influencing extended supply chains will become more and more disruptive. To that end, please consider the following as options to develop your own domestic supply chain.

The Power in Production Management

Efficient Communication and Coordination

When supply-chain partners are closer, it facilitates faster and more effective communication, reducing delays and enhancing coordination in production. Localized supply chains bypass some of the barriers inherent to distributed supply chains, such as language, time zone differences, unreliable foreign communication and power infrastructure, or the continually changing geopolitical landscape.

Quality Control and Consistency

Closer oversight allows for better control over product quality and consistency, as production processes can be monitored more closely, and adjustments made promptly. Proximity makes it easier to manage the quality and consistency of the product.

Flexibility and Responsiveness

Domestic supply chains are often more agile, enabling quicker responses to change in demand, market conditions, or unforeseen events, leading to enhanced overall production flexibility. Again, I harken back to 2020 when all supply chains were thrown into chaos. The U.S. manufacturing complex performed a nearly miraculous pivot to begin producing PPE, ventilators, and other devices and supplies that became critical needs for the medical community and the country at large. Companies whose traditional customer base was shut down realized the need, and their ability to provide the products to meet the need, all while their foreign supply chain lay decimated.

Economic Impact

Job Creation

A robust domestic supply chain supports local employment, contributing to the economic growth of the country and fostering a sense of community well-being. One aspect of a domestic supply chain is the number of new customers that are created by keeping resources nearby. As resources are transferred locally, the purchasing ability and requirements of local businesses and consumers are increased, stimulating more economic activity.

Stimulated Economic Activity

The circulation of money within the domestic economy stimulates economic activity, benefiting not only the supply chain participants but also related industries and businesses. The economic multiplier of a spend with a foreign supplier is zero. The economic multiplier of a spend with a manufacturing company is between 1.5 and 2.4. If you consider the number of raw materials and components that are imported and could be provided domestically, that number could increase substantially.

Skills Development and Training

Investing in local talent development and training programs can contribute to the growth of skilled labor, creating a positive impact on the community and the workforce. As supply chains consolidate, suppliers' accountability continues to progress and remain competitive in cost and quality, raising the standard for all. A result of this is the need to develop talent as companies deploy new technology and innovate to maintain competition.

Sustainability

Large corporations are becoming more public in their environmental, social and governance policies. Some are starting to publish their sustainability reports, and investors are starting to include sustainability efforts in their decisions on where to allocate their capital. When considering sustainability in totality, here are some things you can use as you are courting larger companies as customers:

Reduced Carbon Footprint

The reduced transportation requirements in a domestic supply chain result in lower carbon emissions, contributing to environmental sustainability and reducing the overall ecological impact. Additionally, the energy consumed during manufacturing processes domestically typically will be generated in facilities producing lower carbon emissions than in developing economies.

Resource Efficiency

Close proximity enables better resource management, reducing waste and promoting more efficient use of materials throughout the supply chain. This increased use of domestic resources is also a driver for innovation in material processing and transformation. Further, this includes reduced transportation costs and risk as well as minimizing the geopolitical risks.

Support for Sustainable Practices

As consumer preferences continue to generate demand for eco-friendly products, a domestic supply chain provides a platform for implementing and supporting sustainable and environmentally friendly practices, improving the company's position in the marketplace as a strong corporate citizen which responds to the consumer.

Community Engagement and Support

A domestic supply chain can strengthen ties with local communities, fostering positive relationships and encouraging corporate social responsibility (CSR) initiatives. Long-term sustainability for any business depends on good corporate citizenship. Local supply chains force companies to interact with the community and consider their reputation in all they do.

In summary, a domestic supply chain offers advantages in terms of efficient production management, economic development, social engagement, and sustainability. These benefits collectively contribute to the resilience and well-being of local communities while addressing environmental concerns and promoting responsible business practices.

The Advantage of Applied Technology

Undoubtedly, you are aware of significant changes in technology, especially those that make the news. Many of them have not been applied to mainstream commercial applications yet, but you do need to be aware of them and how they can assist. Having worked with hundreds of manufacturing companies of all sizes, a key to identifying technology that can be added to your operations is knowing what problem it will solve.

When a company is evaluating technology, there are several areas that need to be considered, not in any particular order. First, what infrastructure is required? Consider if any hardware can be acquired locally. Can you use local resources for support? Does the solution require internet access? Wired or wireless?

Second, what personnel do you need to optimize the solution? Do you have someone on the team that would be able to use the system, provide internal support, and train others? Are there external resources you can leverage? You certainly want a partner to help implement the solution, but continuing support is critical for continued success.

Third, what options exist? Consider not only multiple vendors for the solution, but also other options that may use other technologies or be non-technical. Many times, the simplest solution may not be implementing a technology solution at all, but a process change.

Finally for this abbreviated list, make sure you can quantify the desired outcomes. This is often the hard part, especially for technology in the office. On the shop floor, it is much easier to track the amount of time saved on a process to determine ROI. In the office, such performance metrics usually don't exist. It is worth the effort to calculate the effort needed for any process you are examining for change, especially when you are introducing technology. Understanding the effort gives you the baseline for the future state of improvements.

Like every long-term investment, there is a great deal of due diligence and effort to select and implement technology. However, those companies that have selectively applied the technology that addresses a need and fits their company consistently gain competitive advantage.

Technology has been applied successfully across the enterprise to increase efficiency and decision-making quality, and to promote clearer communication. As you evaluate options for applying technology, consider the following:

Do Not Fear to Redesign a Job

Because much of the benefit that technology provides is framed in the number of labor hours saved, or the time that can be redirected to other tasks, it is common for technology projects to generate rumors that people are going to lose their jobs. Especially as AI and machine learning continue to mature and find their practical application in business, people fear jobs will be replaced by technology. However, with a look at combining AI capabilities and the parts of the job that require the human touch, jobs can be redesigned to leverage both and increase service levels, not reduce labor. When adding technology, don't just ask what time can be saved, also ask: "What will this enable the team to do to better serve our customers and help them solve their problems?"

By making service improvement and employee retention priorities for any technology project, you are not driven to make the mistake of seeing employees as expendable, but rather as assets to be developed.

Shop Floor Applications

Robotics

Robotics is often the first application people consider. However, robotics are often misunderstood. Successful robotics installations don't require complex multi-axis movement. Many single-purpose robots have been deployed to improve the production process and quality. One example is pick-and-place robots that retrieve a component from a standardized package and place it for processing (think of picking up a bottle and placing it on a filling machine).

Additions to Current Machines

CNC machines are continually advancing capabilities. A machine that may have been used to perform a single task 5 years ago can now be fitted with an attachment that can perform another task that currently is done manually. This technology reduces material movement and increases quality. It also frees up capacity at what may have been a production bottleneck.

Machine Monitoring

Robotics and increasing capabilities on a production machine allow the worker who performs a manual task to be trained for a higher-level position as operator of the new equipment. These additions also allow for one operator to be productive on multiple machines at the same time. Furthermore, there are many manufacturers that have adopted these technologies and created around-the-clock manufacturing that involves skilled workers setting up the machines and walking away as production continues, even after the lights are turned out. However, to make this model successful, detailed machine monitoring needs to be deployed.

Integrating with sensors on the machine, data can be captured to record not only completed production but also operating conditions. Key temperature, pressure, or electrical data points can be captured. This not only gives a picture of production, but also of the production environment. The data captured then becomes valuable in predictive analytics for identifying leading indicators of problems that will stop the machine and halt production. Since the machines only provide value when they are running, this provides the tools necessary to support continuous production.

Back Office Applications

Integrated Process Automation

Surprisingly, many manufacturing and component parts assembly & redistribution distribution companies require manual processes to move critical data through the organization. Paper copies of documents are passed from office to office for review and approval. Much of the workflow simply requires an initial and there is no comprehensive review. Others that fall outside normal operating parameters require more review, additional approval, and processing. However, identifying these transactions in a paper environment requires another step performed by a human.

As a subset of business process management, integrated process automation provides the toolset to let technology connect data points, identify exceptions, and route those items that need additional attention to the appropriate party. At the same time, the documents that fall within predetermined parameters are processed through the different business management systems or ERP systems through cloud-enabled integration. Moving such non-value add activities away from humans and giving workers opportunities to use their judgment and training increases output and employee contribution.

Business Activity Monitoring

While integrated process management focuses on documents and workflow processes, business activity monitoring targets operational results that fall outside the acceptable range of results. As operations continue, and key milestones such as ship dates, sales volume, and customer balances appear to be outside the acceptable range, presenting this data as a proactive alert brings immediate attention to the condition and allows a response to prevent it or mitigate subsequent effects.

Identifying the issues as they develop gives management the opportunity to take appropriate action instead of being reactive and continually "fighting fires." The result is increased satisfaction not just from the stakeholders, but also from the employees because they see the contribution they are making.

Data Analytics

We discussed data ownership earlier; however, the importance of increasing data analytics cannot be overstated. With more and more data available, understanding the trends, exceptions, and stories the data contains is a key to competitive advantage. Having insight into those future conditions you need to prepare for enables better decision making and more timely decisions that look further into the future, positioning a company for success.

Artificial Intelligence

A quick note on artificial intelligence: There are others who provide detailed analysis and insights on the future of artificial intelligence. For my purpose, I will only recount the technologies above now include, or will soon be enabled by, artificial intelligence. Understanding how to appropriately apply artificial intelligence in an ethical and sustainable manner will be key to successfully navigating technology in the future.

Understand Data Ownership

According to Fortune Business Insights, the cloud computing market was valued at approximately $569.31 billion dollars in 2022 and is forecasted to expand to $2,432 billion by 2030. Cloud computing offers several advantages to businesses and end users alike. Access anywhere, anytime, from any device keeps the information flow always up and presents users with real time data to work with, all without having to manage the infrastructure.

When Web 2.0 came to be, it was based on allowing individuals to create content that was shared across the internet. The platforms used for sharing allowed creators to monetize their contributions. However, the vast majority of the revenue generated by the platforms stayed with the platforms. They targeted individuals based on the data they gathered from links, follows, mentions, and shares. Still today, the platforms own the data.

Data ownership is a new concern that needs to be understood as companies begin to use SaaS solutions to run their businesses. It is common practice by cloud computing companies to assert ownership of client data. This allows them to use the data for internal analytics, and recently, to sell data analytics as a service. Using the data generated by their customers, they can aggregate the data into a large data lake across many companies and industries. As part of the license agreement, the customer agrees to allow this access. Cloud companies are strictly applying the requirement since their business model depends on continuously controlling the data.

As artificial intelligence proliferates and relies on access to large amounts of data to support machine learning and continual advancement, even more ethical concerns arise. The following is a sample of issues that need to be understood and addressed as cloud computing and AI continue to advance:

1. Transparency and Informed Consent
2. Data Control and Access
3. Data Portability
4. Data Privacy
5. Intellectual Property Protection

As the future advances, technology is going to continue to outpace our ability to understand and synthesize the complete picture. Being well informed and building your own framework for managing technology as it applies to your life and business will be critical.

The Labor Relations Struggle

Ever since value-add work has been performed, there has been the management/labor struggle. Some companies have valued their employees and enjoyed a mutually prosperous relationship. These companies often have engaged employees because of mutual respect. Often in bad times they don't lay off employees, and in return, the employees concede some benefit. These are successful companies.

I have personal experience with a second-generation family business where the third generation had no interest in continuing to operate the company. The owner valued his employees and realized their efforts helped build a successful company. He felt he had a responsibility to each of them, so he willed the company to an employee stock ownership plan (ESOP) when he passed. Now, the employees are benefiting from the company they helped build.

On the other hand, you only have to read the accounts of building the Hoover Dam, the early meat packing industry, or the railroad to learn why labor unions were formed (and ultimately became powerful), and appreciate that the struggle is real. Companies that treat employees as a consumable resource still exist today; however, employees' physical mobility and the plethora of opportunities lead to underperformance.

Having worked with hundreds of companies over my career, there are two common threads present in this latter type of company: hubris and greed. Hubris and ego set leadership on a higher plane than the employees, in a position of condescension and disdain, making it impossible for the employees to contribute. I once had a CEO tell me, "I have 25 employees, which means I have 25 headaches." This man had to close one of his businesses and take a substantial financial loss because he was unwilling to listen to his employees and realize he had made a strategic mistake. He continued to lose money for years until the conditions became unsustainable, in all appearances because of hubris.

In addition, greed often tints leadership's views so employees are viewed as transactions and not partners. Valuing the employees you lead and recognizing their contributions will create greater opportunities for you.

Create and Maintain an Engaging Work Environment

Some of you reading this, and some of the small business owners you know, think: "When someone gets hired, they agree to give a fair day's work and I agree to pay a fair day's wage. As long as we both keep our agreement, there shouldn't be a problem, and that will keep the doors open."

I won't disagree on the mutual contract. And, if the world worked according to Frederick Taylor where the best employees are breathing robots, that would be the solution. However, business is complex. People's attitudes and expectations have changed.

The truth is, if you don't allow the talent you have on your team to participate, develop, and explore opportunities, your competition will. When things opened up after the 2020-2021 lockdown, companies struggled to find workers. Turnover was high because the workforce wasn't willing to go back to the same-old same-old. Those attitudes continue. You need to accept it.

If people aren't lining up to fill your vacant positions, why not? Are you giving them a reason to feel they are important? Are you giving them a vision of what they can be? You have to provide more than a paycheck now.

Keeping your employees engaged and committed to moving your company forward, by giving them opportunities to contribute outside their normal tasks, is a no-money-down investment. It is found money when they share their ideas for improving your business.

Much has been written about the attitude of the younger worker and how it has changed from the Baby Boomer generation. The Internet has provided tools for the Millennials and Generation Z that were unimaginable 40 years ago. Today you can go online and with enough time you can master nearly any subject. This unfettered access to the tools for self-learning has decreased the status of long-term employees as experts in a subject. You now have to prove you know the subject, not just say you do and expect younger employees to follow along.

Related to this, younger employees look for continual challenges. Requiring an employee to continue to perform the same task on a regular basis will lead to disengagement, low morale, and ultimately increased employee turnover. Providing challenges for the employees that allow them learning opportunities, advancement opportunities, and opportunities for self-promotion is necessary.

Additionally, employees expect the companies they're working for to create an environment where employees hold some key values, and they expect their employer to share them.

First and foremost, is what I call "stakeholdership". For better or for worse, in a climate of economic instability, income inequality, and political imbalances, employees view themselves as either stakeholders or expendable. those who view themselves as stakeholders give the organization time, commitment, and their minds actively trying to advance the organization they work for. Those who view themselves as expendable give less than 60% of their energy, will, and emotional commitment toward growing your business.

Creating a culture where employees willingly go above and beyond for the company is counterintuitive to many efficiency models and productivity strategies. But one question you need to ask, when considering investing in employees, is one of the most overlooked questions in business: What is the cost of replacing people?

Each employee you retain through investment saves you lost productivity, hiring expenses, training expenses for the new employee, lost productivity until the new employee becomes competent, and increased unemployment taxes due to high turnover. Ancillary to that, companies with high turnover tend to have a less acceptable safety record, which increases insurance costs. Additionally, higher turnover often leads to lower morale of remaining staff as their workload increases, and leads to reputation risk as people who leave express their opinion of your company.

Second, and this is critical: your employees expect you to provide opportunities for them to grow. They expect opportunities to grow professionally, personally, socially, and financially. They expect you to support their social causes, to express shared values, and to be completely transparent in all things that affect them.

Additionally, younger employees expect you to provide them with the tools that will enable them to be successful at their job. Because the younger generation has grown up with and only known internet technology and access to a world of information, you must provide them with current technology, networks of resources they can tap into when they're looking for answers, and the empowerment to use those tools.

The vast majority of employees want to do a good job for their employer. They want to feel good at the end of a workday that they accomplished something. It is imperative that they understand their impact by doing their job correctly.

As a leader, it is your responsibility to understand the value of each position to the organization and to external stakeholders. If you are not giving your employees a chance to express ideas on new processes, community impact, new markets to pursue, new products, etc., you are missing out.

Formal Education's Failure to Prepare

Out of school less than a year, with a freshly minted CPA certificate, I recall sitting across the desk from a company owner and telling him he was making a financial and legal mistake. This was uncharted territory for me. None of the classes I took getting my bachelor's degree in finance, nor the additional accounting courses, prepared me for this. The coursework helped me to become very good at financial accounting and analysis, cost accounting, auditing—those things they call the hard skills. But in the real world, the things that make the most difference are communication, understanding personal bias and tendencies, as well as motivations and use of power.

It wasn't until I met Darryl Vernon Poole that the importance of developing these "untaught" skills became vividly real.

So what are the charges I would lay against the formal education I, and it seems many others, received? We'll examine them in the following sections.

Information is Not Being Put in Context to Help Understand Its Importance

A classic example of this was in my business communications class. We learned the proper format for a business letter—date on line one, an inch of white space, the address of the person we are writing to, the salutation, opening paragraph, body to support the opening paragraph a closing with a salutation and signature. Form was taught over function.

We learned how to create the communication; we did not learn to communicate. We never learned about the different ways people receive and process information. We never learned how to consider the goals of the message and the audience we were sending it to. Since the receiver's perception of the problem and how it aligns with the message we are sending affects the outcome, knowing how to meld the two is critical for proper communication.

Skills to Deal with a Messy World are Not Taught because of Comfort

This particular failure does not lie entirely upon education, but as a place where we should expand our horizons, be exposed to divergent viewpoints, learn to debate and exercise our curiosity. More and more we don't discuss differing viewpoints. We live in a social-media-created echo chamber that makes any opposing view taboo. Further, people are easily offended. More and more people are expressing their right not to be offended, so we don't consider opposite points of view and can't engage in meaningful discourse.

In business, and society in general, progress is driven by collaboration and cooperation. Sometimes that means working with people that hold opposite, maybe even controversial, points of view. How do we deal with that?

I remember a project team for a class, which had a member the others didn't know how to relate to. He was outside their normal social group and had a completely different background, and his point of view was disruptive to the other three in the group. When the three like-minded students went to the instructor about it, the instructor's response was "Work it out." No advice, no questioning for clarification. This was a perfect opportunity to teach how to work through conflict. Instead, the professor chose to sidestep the responsibility.

If higher education is going to help make students successful, they need to make development of the total person a priority; that includes instruction on decision making in a world of opposing and incomplete data. Expanding and developing curiosity leads to a more capable person, because they will have a greater context to consider in all cases.

Additionally, helping students develop coping skills for the situations they will face in the workplace—such as incomplete information, values conflict, performance expectations, and lack of clear direction by leadership—will better prepare them for what lies ahead.

Not Teaching Skills to Understand Social and Organizational Dynamics

There is a common theme in these critiqiues: the lack of developing non-quantitative skills. Regardless of how well supported and how valid the analysis is, unless the person presenting the results has the ability to frame them to account for the dynamics of the organization and the audience, the odds that the message will result in the desired outcome are slim. The lack of training on interpersonal and organizational dynamics is hindering great ideas from being considered and implemented.

There is an inherent risk to including these skills in a quantitative course: not developing the analytical skills to the fullest. However, I believe it is easier to teach quantitative skills than qualitative. Perhaps forgoing some of the quantitative for the sake of building a skillset in communication and collaboration might be beneficial.

Selling Critical Thinking Itself as a Product of Any Major
In the past ten years or so, I have work more with people who graduated with a liberal arts degree, and I have noticed a concerning trend. Regardless of the degree, they all say that one of the things they learned is critical thinking. However, their decision-making and overall thought processes are dominated by bias and exclusion. It makes me wonder if they believe they have critical thinking skills only because they were told they were being taught such.

Critical thinking is a very desirable skill and we need more of it across society, which makes it an attractive outcome of education. However, it seems what is being passed off as critical thinking is teaching that the only correct view is one that accepts the professor's view on the major critical social theories. While understanding these theories, including their development and application, are important, framing critical thinking in such a limited focus really is a bait-and-switch.

According to Oxford's dictionary, critical thinking is defined as, "the objective analysis and evaluation of an issue in order to form a judgment." Developing a framework for evaluation and decision making on objective analysis is a key requirement for success and promotion in business as well as helping society in general. Charlie Munger talked about a "lattice of mental models" to use in decision making. Across the multitude of businesses, across multiple generations and across all ethnicities, these evaluative and decision making skills are lacking. If "critical thinking" is a product of formal education, either the definition needs to be changed, or the education system is failing.

Younger People have Incorrect Expectations of Their Job

It is common to follow stories in news media, institutional studies, academic studies, and over-flowing interviews concerning the general dissatisfaction and stresses of young people with their career potential, economic future, and working conditions. Graduating college with an unprecedented amount of student debt and the prospects of having to work for years before seeing substantial wage growth is certainly disconcerting. However, the marketplace has not changed. It rewards the value produced, not entitlement because of your economic and social status. Young people are entering the workplace not understanding this principle, and it is causing issues in the workplace, which we will discuss later.

There is an Increase in the Inability to Manage Conflict and Uncertainty

While the increased rejection of opposing views is not entirely a result of the formal education system, the bias of many professors is influencing students' ability to deal with opposing views and manage conflict. A beautiful outcome of collaboration is the give and take between parties, the negotiation and acceptance of each other. However, collaboration and cooperation are often set aside because of differing social views. The initial reaction is to disregard the other party and proclaim them unreasonable, which disrupts the communication channels. There has been an increase in workplace conflict, according to a Myers-Briggs study:

> "And compared to the company's 2008 study, workplace conflict is becoming more common. Over a third (36%) of people

now reported dealing with conflict often, very often, or all the time, compared to 29% previously."[3]

(https://www.themyersbriggs.com/en-US/Programs/Conflict-at-Work-Research)

This increase in conflict has several negative effects, as we will examine later.

There is a Lack of System Thinking to Identify Relationships, Causation and Correlation

While the technical skills are being taught, the ability to analyze situations in the greater context and make an objective evaluation and recommendation are often lacking. New graduates are very capable in determining the quantitative results of business cases. However, they are lacking the applications knowledge to put those results in context of what a business has to accomplish to "Keep the Doors Open!" Without practicums and upper-class and Masters-level college mentorships, it is significantly difficult for present students to articulate a narrative that explains what their results mean under in the current conditions.

Please bear in mind that these above factors sit in the middle of a world in constant turmoil from domestic and global conflicts, geopolitical upheavals, social change, and global an array of global uncertainties. In every direction there is a prescience of uncertainty.

Consider: How are the combination such matters affecting the workplace? There is a general increase in mental health issues. According to the World Health Organization:

"Globally, an estimated 12 billion working days are lost every year to depression and anxiety at a cost of US$ 1 trillion per year in lost productivity."[4]

(https://www.who.int/news-room/fact-sheets/detail/mental-health-at-work)

Consider Further: Mental Health America's 2023 Workplace Wellness Research report observation

"In 2022, 81% of workers report that workplace stress affects their mental health, compared to 78% of respondents in 2021."

(https://www.mhanational.org/2023-workplace-wellness-research#:~:text=In%202022%2C%2081%25%20of%20workers,friends%2C%20or%20co%2Dworkers.)

When people are put into an environment where there is a misalignment of expectations, lack of clear communication, injustice real or perceived, and conflict, stress is a natural outcome. Increased stress is taking its toll on today's workers. Businesses are seeing lost productivity increase. Because businesses must continue to produce, lost time from one team member then causes increased work on others to meet the business goals, increasing stress on those team members and compounding the problem.

Increased Bias against the Corporate / Work Environment
An increasing number of workers are entering the workforce with a bias against the corporate environment and corporations. Whether it is because they see corporate profits at record levels, read of corporate corruption, resent corporate influence in politics, or see corporations as destroyers of the planet, this slant shades perceptions going into the workforce.

While the perception that corporations are evil is not solely a result of the formal education system, it is interesting that a Gallup survey finds the majority of people with some college education, a bachelor's degree, or graduate degree have a negative feeling of corporations.[5]

This slant brings with it an underlying distrust and the relationship is shaded from the beginning. Combined with other beliefs and thinking patterns previously discussed, it creates challenges in the workplace that must be overcome for a long-term relationship of trust and cooperation to exist.

Increased Number of Creators with a Small Percentage Of Success

As more and more workers enter the marketplace with a bias against a corporate environment, and hear reports of workplace stress and consider the economic inequality between executives and workers, more and more turn to individual content creation as a way to make a living. However, few find a niche where they can be seen as an expert. Their lack of life experience limits their ability to provide value in the marketplace. The results are an increased number of creators, with a large percentage failing to build an income stream sufficient to support themselves.

In their study on online creators, Linktree, a company helping online creators manage their content, reports:

> "Only 12% of full-time creators earn more or around $50K a year, while 46% of creators earn less than $1K in annual revenue."[6]

They also found:

> "Studies show that a YouTuber with 20,000 views per day and an average click-through rate of 50% earns only a little over the US poverty line of $13,590."[7]

As people face the hard realities of the creator economy, the lack of success and increased workload to advance their personal online brand are leading to burnout and poor mental health. According to StreamHatchet:

"Digital Creators are burning out. 67% of creators are affected by mental health issues which manifest into procrastination, work-life balance struggles, and lesser quality of life." [8]

(https://insights.streamhatchet.com/the-creator-mental-health-report#:~:text=Digital%20Creators%20are%20burning%20out,and%20lesser%20quality%20of%20life).

This condition is putting an increasing number of workers in a precarious position, where they are running out of options to support themselves. Long-term, this has the possibility of developing into a significant economic support issue for governments.

Hubris in Decision-Making

We all want to be right, or conversely, none of us want to be wrong. Many times we tie our identity to how things turn out whenever we make decisions. We want to protect our identity, and that often leads to applying a bias or some other form of hubris that eases our discomfort with the uncertainty we face.

Take, for instance, the owner of a printing company in the Midwest. He built the business with a few customers that represented well over 80% of his total revenue. The customers were the IRS, and three state revenue departments. He learned the process for successfully bidding on the contracts to print and distribute income tax booklets when he first started his company in the mid-1980s. Each year, the number of contracts he won continued to grow, until he produced 85% of all 1040 tax booklets. Since the margin on these contracts was substantial, he contracted for paper and continually purchased additional or upgraded equipment. Much of the equipment sat idle during January through September but ran 24/7 from October through mid-December.

He was confident he had built a never-ending gravy train. Despite pleas from his controller to diversify and pay off some of the equipment debt instead of expanding, he continued to expand and made no substantial efforts to bring in additional customers to use the excess capacity for the first nine months of the year.

Then it happened: in 1996, the printing industry started to feel the initial effects of digitization. The large commercial printers had excess capacity. Their solution to this excess capacity was to bid the tax booklets not with a normal margin, but covering the costs of excess capacity. The gravy train ended. That trend continued until, a few short years later, he was forced to sell to avoid bankruptcy.

His overconfidence and his bias based on past experience blinded him to the shift his competitors were making – a shift caused by the changing markets, something he did not account for, because for him it had been business as usual with presses sitting idle.

While his overconfidence in his abilities led to his downfall, overconfidence in others you trust can cause bad decisions as well. Existing-relationship bias and anchoring bias led to bad decisions for another business owner. He made an investment in a company because a friend asked him to do it as a favor. The friend was selling his company and needed someone to buy the printing division, at an inflated price of course. But in return, he would make sure the buyer was awarded print work at inflated prices to provide a solid return on the investment. Enter the international company that purchased the friend's business. They told the new print shop owner he had 30 days to get his equipment out of their building. "But we have a contract" he protested. Their response: "Sue us and let's see who has more lawyers."

Bias

There are over 180 cognitive biases that lead us to make decisions that ignore facts and context. Over the years, I have observed several of them seem to be most prevalent.

What is the relationship between hubris and these biases? Hubris is the overconfidence we are right. We use these biases to confirm our position and further enhance our confidence. When faced with conflicting information, they are handy tools we have at our ready to defend our position, consciously or subconsciously. Here are the five biases I have seen become most prominent in decision making over the last 10 years.

Bias	Explanation
Optimism Bias	We overestimate our position, particularly if it is the result of personal effort.
Belief Bias	If a conclusion supports your belief, you will rationalize anything that defends it.
Backfire Effect	When your belief is challenged, you believe even more strongly.
Availability Heuristic	Our judgements are most influenced by that which most easily comes to mind.
Confirmation Bias	We search for ways to justify our beliefs.

Overcoming Poor Decision-making

The good news is, we can overcome our hubris and make better decisions. It isn't easy, because we have likely developed specific decision-making muscles through years of practice. I have a process of very elementary steps to help make better decisions and put aside our hubris and bias.

The first step is the hardest: admitting there is a problem. What can we do to find out if there really is a problem? First there must be a willingness to look at ourselves and accept what we find. Without an objective evaluation, we will not uncover what is in our blind spots.

Once you agree self-examination is necessary, start by looking at the past. Make a list of decisions, big and small. What do you remember about them? Where did you get the information to support your decision? Who else did you involve in the decision-making process? Was there ever a point that you changed your mind, or considered changing it? Why?

Ask yourself as many questions as you can think of to find out if it was a truly well supported decision or if you relied on your own confidence and biases. As you look at these decisions, does a pattern evolve? Have you identified a bias or tendency?

Once a bias or tendency toward hubris has been identified, take pains to create and to maintain a system that will help you to avoid it in future decisions.

Misaligned Objectives Make for Poor Partnerships

If two people begin walking down different paths, eventually they are not walking together. The evolution of a business relationship between a larger company and a small business often follows this example. As the companies' objectives begin to diverge, usually the larger company develops leverage over the smaller, and the relationship changes, often to the detriment of the small company.

Corporate Conditions

Objectives at the corporate level are created with a different perspective than in a small business. They can be at different levels of the organization, but each difference brings another complication to the relationship. Because they are judged by the market for their short-term performance, corporate actions are meant to enhance the quarterly performance, sometimes at the expense of the longer term. This brings a much sharper focus on each transaction and blurs the view of the relationship.

As a tool to increase employee commitment to the short-term objectives, larger companies create incentive plans for individuals that provide personal gain for meeting the objectives. These plans reframe the business relationships into a series of transactions instead of a long-term partnership. Larger companies have a very good understanding of the superpower of incentive, and leverage it to their advantage when possible.

Because larger companies have access to a broader selection of suppliers and customers, they are less affected by negative actions of a single company. They leverage this as a risk management tool and sometimes as leverage with a smaller business.

SMB Conditions

Small businesses have objectives also. Typically these objectives reflect the owner's values and goals. They are often more personal and longer term. The timeframe for these objectives often puts them in direct competition with the larger company. Let's look at a few of these objectives.

Smaller companies struggle to compete with the lowest price. They are cost conscious, but have little leverage with suppliers since most of their suppliers are larger. Often, being the low-price leader is not the image the owner wants to develop. They believe in providing a higher level of service and being compensated for it. The focus on service as a differentiator moves the company away from providing the lowest cost.

When a small business starts, there is likely a strong relationship with several customers who can support the business as it develops. This reliance on strong relationships continues to be a key value going forward. However, because relationships are with people and not with corporations, the cycle of people moving in and out of positions that a smaller company interacts with makes it hard to create the meaningful relationships that smaller businesses seek.

Because small business owners hold a deep responsibility to their employees, they are concerned about continuing to support them. They want to make sure the business can continue to contribute to their community, and they understand how devastating it can be when a business closes. This often causes them to accept unfavorable terms put upon them by larger organizations.

Examples of Conflicting Objectives

Let's take a look at some of the most common requirements larger companies have placed upon their smaller business counterparts. All of the examples come from companies I have worked with over my career.

Required Cost Decreases

Big box retailers as well as high volume buyers in manufacturing use heavy handed tactics to require small suppliers to reduce the purchase price each year. Wal-Mart, famous for their price rollbacks, is well known for pushing the rollback cuts to the supplier to enable a steady margin on the items.

With little leverage on suppliers to provide cost decreases on raw materials, the small business is in a difficult position: walk away from the business, or reduce their own margin and profitability to support their larger customer.

Extended Payment Terms for Large Customers

A Forbes article from 2019 details how larger companies systematically pay a small company's invoice after the due date, sometimes up to thirty days later than they pay an invoice from a larger supplier.

One of my clients was concerned about cashflow problems caused by new credit terms with a major customer that allowed 120 days from shipment to pay. The supplier felt compelled to accept the extended terms or they would lose the significant customer. Once the customer secured the extended credit terms, they did give the smaller company more business, but even with the extended terms, they slow-paid the invoices, increasing the negative impact.

Requirement for Increased Service/Investment without Increasing Price

One way that larger companies cut expenses is to pass certain functions to their supply chain without increasing their purchase price. One example: a small supplier to a heavy equipment manufacturer was told that to keep the business, they would need to start stocking a minimum quantity of certain items and guarantee expedited delivery for the customer. The customer then did not increase business with the supplier, so many of the stocked items remained on the shelf well past normal inventory turns, and the supplier was forced to finance this extra inventory.

Another example of this has proliferated with the growth of online commerce. Many larger companies are now passing order fulfillment to the supplier via drop-ship purchase orders. A client in the knock down furniture business has had 300 shipments per month to big box distribution centers replaced by 3000 shipments to individuals on behalf of the retailer. This required substantial changes to warehouse operations, including new staffing and systems to handle the increased number of shipments. However, the cost the big box retailer pays per unit remains the same.

Increased Reporting Requirements to Support Larger Company Objectives

With recent ESG initiatives, larger companies are requiring reporting from their supply chain to support their ESG claims of better control and citizenship across their supply chain. The burden falls on the smaller suppliers to first understand the reporting requirements, then create the reporting mechanism. This additional overhead for the supplier is not increasing profitability and not supporting internal goals. The supplier is not compensated for the additional requirements; it is simply a cost of doing business.

Handling Conflicting Objectives

When these conflicts arise, they need to be handled considering what is most important to each party. When a small business is confronted with a requirement that does not further their objectives, there are different approaches to take in search of a resolution.

If a larger customer produces a new demand on their suppliers, it isn't an accident. It is an action supporting a larger departmental objective which aligns with an overarching company goal. The company goal may be to reduce costs. The first thought is to get concessions from suppliers. However, the PO cost is only part of the total cost of procurement. Transportation, warehousing, and material handling all add to the total cost of a product. You must first understand the true objective before you can decide on the best way to meet it, from both sides of the transaction.

Once the objective is identified, creating alternate solutions that arrive at the same result is a way to test whether you are working with a company that understands the value of a continued relationship versus the cost of onboarding a new supplier. If the goal is to reduce costs by a certain level, perhaps change the way orders are submitted, the way the items are transported, or even how they are fulfilled to the ultimate customer. In each of these alternatives, consider all the cost components on both sides. Perhaps the supplier will begin drop shipping to the end customer, but can increase the sales price on those orders to recover their increased cost?

In the end, if a small business can absorb the loss of a customer, it might be best in the long run to walk away from bad business. Many business owners will tell you the key to their long-term success is staying true to their values and principles. Allowing yourself to be manipulated into a business deal that violates those values is a sure way to lose.

It takes small and large companies working together to make the economy work. As part of a strong long-term strategy, it is important for large companies to understand that while pushing a stronger position may benefit you in the short term, in the long term it hurts your bottom line, not just financially, but in public perception and corporate citizenship, while raising questions of the quality of governance.

The Importance of a Variety of Relationships

We are all familiar with the saying "don't put all your eggs in one basket." We apply diversification to investment strategies, and the value of diversity in teams is well documented. However, because of many small businesses' bent toward long-term relationships, they often cast aside diversity when it comes to customer and vendor business partners.

It seems like common sense not to rely on a small number of external partners (meaning customers and vendors) in your business. There is safety in numbers. The principle of dilution shows that the lower the impact a single party or action can have, the lower the risk to the system.

I once worked for a company where 85% of revenue came from seasonal business with four customers. To compound the risk, 80% of that business came from a single customer. When that customer changed business models, it started an unstoppable death spiral for the company.

The same goes for suppliers. If you have limited options for sourcing products or services, you are at risk and subject to the supplier's power to impact your business.

Everyone has a different perspective. The more points of view you have about what is happening in your industry or the marketplace, the more information you have to make decisions. Working with a diverse group of partners provides a broader perspective that would be difficult to gain as an individual. The world, and even industries, are too large and changing too fast to stay abreast of the changes alone.

One of the most valuable services you can provide to the marketplace is connecting others. Introduce strangers who can make each other better, meet specific needs that advance a cause, or are mutually profitable. This is a power that generates huge value and puts you first in mind as opportunities arise. The quote "Your network is your net worth" has been attributed to many and emphasizes the importance of creating a network to support and to support you.

Building a strong network is also a risk mitigation strategy. A limited number of relationships to rely on exposes you to outside forces with little or no backup and few contingency plans. The more customers and vendors you have that will join you in tough times or times of opportunity, the less risk you face.

Customers

If you concentrate customers to a single or a couple of related industries, any downturn in that business area can have a major impact on your business. As we have seen in the oil and natural gas boom and bust cycle, entire industries can be shut down in a very short time. Companies that supplied the industry also were affected, but those that had relationships outside the industry were better able to weather the downturn. By decreasing volatility, companies are better able to plan and create strategies for more consistent growth.

Imagine, if you will, the opportunity to buy one of two very similar businesses, both in the same industry, selling similar products with similar revenue. Upon closer examination, you find that one derives 85% of its revenue from 4 customers and the other has no customer representing more than 15% of its sales. Which one would hold the higher value? The one with less risk certainly has an advantage.

The more customers you have, the more needs they have. Continual involvement with a broad cross-section of customers will reveal more opportunities.

Vendors

While there is much discussion on diversifying your customer base to create opportunity and mitigate risk, creating a broad array of supplier relationships can add value as well.

The last few years have magnified the fragility of distributed supply chains. Maintaining a number of suppliers, especially when they do not share supply chains, gives you an opportunity to overcome supply chain disruptions like[pandemics, problems with the Panama Canal, strikes at shipping ports, or a lack of shipping containers where you need them.

When you have multiple suppliers you can count on, you have a lever you can pull to create an agreement that helps you meet your objectives. Remember, there is more than the PO cost to consider in the procurement cycle. Vendors all have different strengths and capabilities. Aligning with the ones that best meet your objectives can be your primary focus.

However, to maintain relationships with secondary sources, you can request concessions that compensate for their weaknesses and play to their strengths. Playing to each vendor's strengths will give you coverage for different disruptions.

As suppliers add new products, or hear of opportunities with their other customers, you can be positioned to take advantage of them simply because you have learned of the need.

There is strength in numbers. The broader array of companies you deal with as either a customer or supplier, the more value you can create, the more risk you can avoid, and the more you can help others. Nurturing a variety of relationships is good for business.

Maintain Your Own Panel of Experts

The ever-changing landscape of business has made it nearly impossible to keep current on new regulations, business trends, and technology. To that end, the successful leaders going forward will engage with experts with particular knowledge in domains they are unfamiliar with.

Identifying the subjects where you hold strong opinions but lack sufficient knowledge to make well informed decisions will be key to success. Self-assessment and honest reflection will enable a clear vision of capabilities. Further understanding weaknesses professionally, intellectually, and morally provides the foundation for self-development. Engaging with experts in the fields where weaknesses exist will be key.

A threat has been developing over the past several years that must be addressed. It is increasingly common to surround ourselves with those of a like mind. I believe the echo chamber that is social media has contributed to the idea that dialogue with those who hold contrarian views is no longer required and in fact discouraged. However, to hold an opinion that you can defend, you must understand the alternative position. Seeking the contrarian view is an opportunity to solidify your own opinion and possibly expose a fallacy you are holding on to. Seeking advice you may not agree with is a sign of strong leadership and self-awareness.

How do you find the right people to help you? A good place to start is by talking with the professionals you already work with and trust. Those who want to be a true help have a network of professionals they rely on to fill in their knowledge gaps.

Second, look at professional and industry associations and websites. Who is contributing articles and informing you of trends, and raising questions for your consideration? Is what they are saying resonating with you? That is a potential helper.

Finally, ask your employees. Why did I put them last? To emphasize them. They are often your most valuable resource. They are close to the situation, they have skin in the game, they rely on your success to help them be successful. I can't overstate how valuable your employees can be for you, if you are willing to let them be.

When it comes to building your team of experts, your own board of directors if you will, you certainly want to find the most qualified people to help. But in building your team, don't forget that you have something to offer as well. Help others first and the help you need will find you. There is a universal truth that the help you provide to others will return to you, multiplied. Don't get too caught up in reaching your goals, if that means you don't help someone else reach theirs.

The Small Business Plateau

Michael Gerber, in his classic work *The E-Myth,* coined the phrase, "technician who had an entrepreneurial seizure." He was referring to someone with specific skills who decided to start a business and make more money for themselves. On the surface, it holds just a little derogatory sting, but with a deeper look, that's not the case.

Many small businesses were started by people who wanted a better life. Likely very few of them had any training, education, or experience running a business. They learned on the fly. I would venture a good number would say they weren't prepared for the demands of running a business and the decisions they had to make. Many wondered what they got themselves into at least once or twice. But it was too late, they now had employees with families depending on them.

In *The E-Myth*, Gerber posits that you start a business for one purpose: to sell it. either to yourself or to someone else. Those who start a business and decide to sell it to themselves (or, "Look at what I have built for ME!") often are less strategic and rely less on systems because they enjoy working in the business each day. The business is an integral part of their life. However, this can often create a self-fulfilling "comfort zone" can stifle the active seeking or innovation and opportunity. Which, in the absence of renewable and challenges thinking may in turn lead to the business reaching a certain plateau in revenue, innovation, and vision.

Over my 30+ years helping businesses, I have found there are several root causes for this plateau. After we look at the causes, we will look at the potential outcomes and then how a business can start growing again, after resting on the plateau for a time.

As mentioned earlier, one of the primary reasons a business grows to a certain level and stays there is the lack of focus on planning, strategy and systems. Oftentimes, business owners are busy working in the business, managing the day to day, putting out fires, responding to new opportunities and such; they don't spend the time in long-term planning, strategic development, or creating systems that enable consistent quality results.

Eventually, the company grows to a point that the lack of these long-term levers becomes a hindrance and the business just can't grow anymore without collapsing on itself. Because the owner and the team have developed their own specific processes and silos of data, onboarding new employees is difficult and results start to suffer.

Long-term planning and consistent processes are tools to prevent an early business plateau. If we step back and consider our craftsman starting their own enterprise, their lack of training and knowledge about running a business often holds them back. Craftsmen are very good at what they do, and they hold immense expertise in their chosen trade. However, they may not understand financing covenants, inventory turns, and financial ratio analysis. They can certainly educate themselves, but this sometimes comes too late.

Another thing to consider: the plateau may be planned. To use a phrase from Grant Beresford, a prominent sales leader, many are "lifestyle" entrepreneurs. They have built the business to the point they have sold it to themselves. They are reaping the rewards of their years of labor, getting the income from the business to allow them a certain lifestyle. They are content. If the business were to grow substantially, it would affect the lifestyle they enjoy, so they put the business in maintenance mode to keep it running.

The final cause we will look at is something most small businesses have to face: lack of resources. Regardless of where you get your information, you will likely hear that insufficient capital is the most common reason businesses fail.

In addition to business failure, lack of capital is a hindrance to growth. If a company does not have the financial resources to take advantage of opportunities, the ability to expand and grow is limited. The importance of financial stability cannot be overstated.

It is inevitable that changes in the business lifecycle will cause different outcomes. Here we will discuss some of the outcomes when a business enters a period of flat growth. They can all be overcome, but you will likely face one or more of them. Be aware they might come, and understand they are part of the process.

One of the most effective competitive advantages a business can have is to be in position to take advantage of opportunities that arise. This is a broader truth across all of life. The stronger your position, the more resilient and sustainable you can be. When a business plateaus, the ability to take advantage of new opportunities diminishes. The inertia of the plateau is a hindrance to changing or adapting the business. As the missed opportunities pile up, the competitive position will erode, and the business will move from plateau to decline.

The nature of a free market provides very few businesses the ability to survive without continual growth. If a business stays on a plateau long enough, market forces will cause a business to start to contract. Eventually sales, services, employee morale, and profitability will decline. Then the death spiral starts.

There are many factors that determine how long a company can stagnate before the decline starts and how long it can survive the decline. However, it is part of the cycle.

As companies that at one time had a strong market presence start to plateau, the marketplace sees an opportunity to replace them. New entrants with resources that let them be more agile will create competition, forcing everyone in the market to respond or suffer. Businesses that have plateaued and are not looking for ways to expand their presence are at risk of falling behind.

Often, in the case of a planned plateau, a unique circumstance develops. Throughout the business lifecycle, the company brand likely has been built around the owner. They become the company brand. When they then decide to back away from the business or sell it, a substantial amount of the company value walks away with the sale.

Plateaus are part of a normal business lifecycle. Some last longer and the causes vary; however, there are things you can do to help move past them. Here are a few ideas to consider as you look to move past the plateau.

Looking to other industries' business models may be a way to adapt a practice that will provide you with a competitive advantage and start climbing from the plateau. It provides a new perspective on business and inspires the next great idea.

Recently, I talked to an increasing number of business leaders who are joining formal groups of business owners from a variety of industries. They share problems they are dealing with and answer questions among the group. There are differing views on the issue provided by the different experiences and business models. These perspectives can change the lens through which to view the problem.

The business world is more complex than ever. New government regulations, continual tax law changes, and pressures and requirements from customers mount and challenge our ability to stay the course created during our strategic planning session. The universe of knowledge grows exponentially. What new technologies can we apply? How do we keep employees engaged? What about the upcoming talent gap that AI and machine learning are going to create?

You can read plenty of articles online and get a high level of understanding of these issues, and maybe even become well versed in one or two. But without expert advice on these topics you may not be able to optimize the results. Don't be afraid to use the experts available to you. Yes, it costs money, but what will happen if you don't invest in your company?

In addition to getting outside advice, take time to project the future under different scenarios. What will the business look like next year, in three or five years if things don't change? Will you reach the goals you have? What will cause you to come up short? Can you identify what the problem is? Not having enough sales isn't the problem, it is a symptom.

One way to find a way forward is to look at the problems your customers and your customer's customers are facing. How can you solve those problems? This is your competitive advantage. It will strengthen your relationships, and position you as the expert in the field, someone to look to for help.

Businesses operations are cyclical and generally can be predicted. When a business reaches a plateau, there are options, and those options vary depending on the cause of the plateau and the desired outcome. However, understanding the relationship between the cause and the desired outcome is crucial. You may need to lean on others to help you see that relationship objectively and holistically. You have resources available if you are willing to use them.

Summary

I have covered a good deal in this chapter. We've discussed what it's going to take to be successful going forward. Now let's take a look at action items to implement some of these concepts.

First: take an honest look at your team. I start with the team, because it is usually where you can make the smallest adjustments and see the greatest return. Do you know what is important to them? Do you know their dreams? Do you know what talents they have, that you can let them develop as part of making the business successful? Are you giving them a place they want to come to every day and give you an honest day's work for an honest day's pay?

Second: does your strategic plan include making your technology a lever that can give you oversized results? A common argument against implementing technology is the cost. It does take an investment to get the proper technology implemented in a way that gives you the required returns. I challenge you to identify the areas where technology can help. Take an honest look at your technology. If you are running the same software as you were in 2000, you have accumulated a great deal of technical debt, and it has to be paid if you are going to be in business for the long term.

Third: As you evaluate options to further build, adapt and help prosper your organizations, be sure to incorporate the impact of the following:

Institutional

1. Societal differences threaten mature small business, particularly the increased retirements of 'baby boomers.'
2. Managerial distaste for, and fear of, stronger accountability threatens its own competitive position as well as business sustainability.
3. Lack of evolving institutional structure leads to unmet expectations for both employer and employees—at all levels.

Operational

1. The breadth of "as a service" offerings will continue to increase, putting pressure on operations, net cash management, and changing capital budgeting needed to compete, let alone grow.
2. Technology will continue to accelerate the use of temporary contract labor is replacing unskilled-labor employees. Will this 'detachment' from the production employee generate sufficient energy to rethink automating unskilled production positions?
3. A.I. has already impacted what you do – and will increasingly pressure your client base, your competition, and your planning & reporting functions (human resources, procurement, finance & accounting, regulatory reporting, risk analyses, etc.).
4. Increased quality concerns from offshore production will provide increased manufacturing opportunities for those domestic enterprises determined to better manage quality, costs, and employee opportunities.

Fourth and final note: what is your strategy to make sure you secure your supply chain? To me, that is the most critical risk we face. If you buy from distributors, what are they doing to secure their supply chain? If you can't get the materials, you can't leverage your strengths to serve your customers. Identify the weak links in the supply chain and create a stronger system.

Chapter Six

Managing the Supply Chain of Our Turbulent and Changing World: The Next Steps

W. Keith Story

In this chapter, I want to inform business leaders, and those who mentor them, of some areas they need to consider as they take the reins of social leadership, global business, and economic development across the world. My observations are rooted in my 15 years of experience as a supply chain practitioner and my second career as a marketing and supply chain university professor. This chapter is written from the context of a person that is past the threshold of the under 40 crowd, but not as seasoned as the old guard—therefore I think I am well-suited to be a bridge between these two important, yet distinct groups.

My practitioner experience is largely along the supply chain/marketing interface, and as a result, my observations are focused in this area. Likewise, my experience as a business school professor with a close proximity to first-generation college students (both personally and professionally), and those who will likely populate the non-executive roles in firms, has provided me an opportunity to observe that element of our student population.

As this chapter progresses, I will organize my observations in a way that will allow the reader to internalize them more deeply and use this information to inform their own opinions and actions as they develop strategies to lead the businesses of the future.

As I elaborate on my observations, I will address:

- What I think we are facing in the near-term (10-20 years) for each of these concerns
- What influencing factors seem to be inevitable, yet we are unwilling to accept as reality
- Where I think we are headed, based on these factors
- Some things can we do to resolve, or at least adjust, our current trajectory to one that is more sustainable and productive for future generations

My observations and concerns can have some rather large implications over the next couple of decades if not addressed. Most of these, in my experience, will impact how we design and manage our supply chains and interconnected resource networks.

The Importance of Our Interconnected Resource Networks

When I talk about interconnected resource networks, I am referring to the supply chains that provide the resources and materials that enable the production of the goods and services that power the global economy. These networks are comprised of companies and institutions that deliver the raw materials, labor, information, and financing required to keep the world as we know it spinning.

I use the term "interconnected resource networks" because, as revealed during the COVID-19 period (pandemic and endemic), the proper management, design, and development of these systems are critical to our ability to service the businesses, populations, and economies that we have developed across the globe. We are all intimately connected —the turbulence and change that happen to some will eventually impact us all.

I have observed that neither the business academic nor the practitioner communities put enough emphasis on the importance of these interconnected resource networks that drive our economy. I am concerned about this because not paying close enough attention to this critical part of business capability introduces unnecessary risks into these systems. The world has gotten significantly smaller recently, and in the coming decades, business leaders will have to deal with a planet that has become increasingly interconnected and co-dependent with respect to supplying the world with consumable products for its markets.

With respect to these interconnected networks, decisions are sometimes made that neglect longer-term investments needed to develop sustainable, reliable supply networks for the sake of shorter-term shareholder profits. These decisions can be influenced by focusing on metrics valued by profit-seeking shareholders or by individual actors in firms. I have observed that in some firms, internal functions such as marketing and operations are not always aligned to optimize the firm's resource networks. Sometimes specific corporate functions focus on metrics that de-value essential workers, weaken needed relationships in the network, or neglect parts of the consuming public that do not meet certain economic criteria.

Example metrics of focus	Potential problems
Productivity Metrics	Can require focus on throughput only and neglect issues of job stress, employee well-being, or engagement
Supplier cost metrics	Can create transactional relationships in resource network that don't support development of trust or long-term partnerships
Customer value metrics	Can result in ignoring or undervaluing groups of people that are low income or fall outside of mainstream socio-economic demographics.

What are We Facing in the Near Term (10-20 years) with Our Resource Networks?

Given these tendencies of business, I see a turbulent trajectory for our interconnected resource networks.

We are facing a new world where our interdependent resource and commerce networks determine the success or failure of business enterprises. we will face a magnitude of problems face within parts of our interconnected social infrastructures.

The success and/or failure of business enterprises in the near term is increasingly becoming influenced by a firm's understanding of the competitive nature (and importance) of the resource networks that it uses to develop the value it provides its customers.

In the context of the inter-connected networks across the globe that provide the products that drive economies, we are facing a realization that supply chains are increasingly becoming the area of future competition across the globe. Because the world is becoming smaller due to the proliferation of information and communication technologies, the world's populations are becoming more and more exposed to the vast number of products available. This proliferation of both information and products cannot be stopped, and the impact of this new level of consumption will change several factors in the world's ability to serve the demand that is forthcoming. This competition plays out in several contexts and circumstances, such as infrastructure development, industrial capabilities, and labor force development. A smaller world is leading to increased interdependence of supply chains, with more entities realizing that control of supply chains can lead to competitive advantage and greater control over global resources.

One such behavior that I observed during my years as a consultant and in corporate America was that firms frequently strive for *short term gains to achieve profits vs. investing in longer-term capability that is sustainable over time.* I have seen organizations slash supply chain/operational capabilities (labor, materials, service) to achieve quarterly profitability goals. Companies will sometimes make efforts to reduce immediate costs instead of making the hard choice to increase investments that will be beneficial over time, although they may initially reduce potential profit and return on investments. Some examples of these cost reduction efforts include failing to invest in inventory or in making capital improvements, eliminating investment in additional human resources (human capital) or training of individuals, or through reducing the workforce.

A word about human capital: It is very easy for firms to lay off people, cut inventories, raise prices, and reduce service options (this includes customer service and customer choice) all in an effort to change their short-term financial situation, maintain margins, and please stockholders, sometimes at the expense of other stakeholders. I think that sometimes organizations neglect the personal toll it can take when management reduces certain parts of the organization and its capability for the sake of profit. I believe that these types of behaviors by firms are short-sighted, and many firms assume that rebuilding these capabilities is easier than it actually is.

Laying people off, reducing resources available for individuals to do their jobs, and taking the position that the company is in it for the short term versus the long term can have a negative impact on how individual employees invest their time and energy for the success of the organization. Individual employees, by necessity, become much more focused on their own personal short-term opportunities; employees end up staying with companies for shorter and shorter terms, and taking institutional knowledge away as they move from company to company in search of better opportunities. A company that is invested long term in individuals and the markets they serve will retain more employees and more customers.

If our current trajectory is one that discounts the value of fostering and developing great interconnected resource networks, short-term thinking in institutional behavior like this will inherently introduce short-term thinking when it comes to developing these networks.

Supply chain networks and these interconnected resource networks require time and energy to create the physical infrastructure and inter-personal relationships to support the flow of products, information, and money across different economies and across different resource sources. Consider how long it took the ancient Silk Road to develop across China and Central Asia at a time before traditional goods-movement infrastructure existed. Now consider the Belt and Road initiative (the New Silk Road) and the tremendous long-term planning and investment that countries are making as they put together this new set of infrastructure tools to facilitate trade across Asia, Africa, and the rest of the globe. This trade represents our interconnected networks, enabling us to get goods from some of the far reaches of the planet into some of the major economic markets of the world.

To reiterate, short-term investment behavior can be quite dangerous in that it doesn't develop the deep trust, capability, or other requirements needed to have a very robust and resilient network. When firms are looking mainly for low-cost, riskless, minimally embedded resource networks, they will inherently not be resilient. Disruptions in the network will cause a cascade of events that make the entire network unstable.

Such cases can be identified using examples from the COVID-19 pandemic, natural disasters, or infrastructure problems that have resulted in disruptions of flow across the network. Our networks are so tied to efficiency, low investment, and low margins that any stoppage or lack of resources in the system will cause a complete shutdown. Two big things we found out during the pandemic: 1) how interconnected our supply systems really are and the importance of understanding how deep the networks go, and 2) the amount of risk that's inherent in our networks because we wrongly assume they're always going to work.

Another challenge firms have is the **lack of effective alignment between functions that influence a firm's overall supply chain performance.** This introduces risk into a firm's ability to serve customers. Many firms tend to view their supply-chain operations and the marketing/commercial parts of the business as competing entities. Several times in my professional career I saw the operational, manufacturing, and logistics groups viewed as cost centers and not the value-delivery functions of the business that they really are. Additionally, working in inventory management, I saw the distribution leg of the operation being viewed as just the people that take things off shelves and put them in boxes. I think this is a very short-sighted view of the relationships between the sales and marketing groups and the operational logistics/distribution groups.

I think one of the things that is most difficult for a lot of businesses is to envision supply chain as a part of, and an extension of, the organization. If the job of sales and marketing functions are to identify what customers value, then the job of the supply chain—the manufacturing/operational/logistics portion of the organization—is to deliver what the sales and marketing teams promise. Therefore, the two groups should be intimately interconnected whenever and wherever engagement with the customer is required.

This is even more important in the current business environment, given that for many B2B and B2C customers, the last engagement they have with a business supplier is through logistical and distribution services. For many customers, this interaction is manifest in the last-mile capabilities of organizations and increasingly, the last-100-feet capabilities of organizations.

One impactful experience that helped develop my perspective was during my years working in corporate for an industrial metals manufacturer. A project I led was intended to improve delivery reliability and reduce lead times to the customer. During my investigation to understand the causes of the problem, I discovered that there was a disconnect between how much product the customer wanted and how the orders were translated into work for the manufacturing facility.

In an effort to ensure product availability, the customer ordered over 100 tons of material each month. Little did they know that orders of that size required custom runs by the factory, and each run was made on a 12-week cycle. If there were any delays in standard production, the custom product could take even longer.

To solve the problem, I had representatives from the customer procurement team meet with representatives from our sales and manufacturing teams. By having these key groups interact with each other directly, I was able to understand the ordering patterns of our customer, how much material they really needed, and what they were using it for so we could properly plan our manufacturing cycles to better meet their needs, while reducing the demands on our manufacturing system.

This project was significant because it helped our understanding of what our customer valued, which was high-quality material and delivery in such a way that it reduced their storage costs, their ordering costs, and their handling costs. We saved them money and better understood how production volumes and production patterns impacted the overall cost profile of the manufacturing facility. Joining the sales and marketing groups, who understand customer value, with the manufacturing group, who understand the operational capabilities and requirements to make a profit, made for a much stronger relationship between customer and supplier and stronger relationships across the supply chain. These results showed me how partnering manufacturing operations with sales and marketing is a win for everyone. Customers get exceedingly high value and suppliers can extract additional value for themselves.

The overall point is that organizations can thrive and become more competitive, stronger, and more valuable as they more tightly connect their ability to understand customer value with their ability to produce and distribute that value to customers. I believe that having a short-term view and not making the investment to do these things is, over time, going to reduce a firm's competitiveness.

In academic research and as evidenced by practitioners, we are seeing that supply chains are the new competitive ground for organizations. It is not enough to be able to identify value, nor is it enough to be able to produce quality products. A company must be able to *deliver* value to its customers to have a competitive advantage, and it is this competitive advantage that companies will seek in the future. We see it in the redevelopment of the Silk Road, and we see it as companies fight for control of waterways and other distribution systems throughout the globe. It is imperative that firms learn to integrate these parts of the business so that they can remain competitive.

I have also seen firms neglecting the bottom of the pyramid. In many places in business (and society), I have seen organizations focus their efforts on becoming more "efficient," and on consumers (members of society) who have more economic means. Many companies would rather have one customer who can spend $10, vs. having ten customers who can only spend $1. This view of the market drives various decisions that can put low-income consumers at a disadvantage. From food deserts to predatory practices that businesses engage in to take advantage of low-income people, firms are not using their considerable wealth and power to better engage lower-income populations and ensure that they can become larger parts of the consuming public.

Supply chains are increasingly global and are continually becoming more complex due to a variety of factors. One factor is the development of viable labor resources. As firms search the globe for labor markets that can satisfy their need for cheaper labor, it will require that agreements be made with countries that may not have the rules, regulations, or possibly the human rights provisions workers are accustomed to in developed economies. Managing a workforce that spans such a diverse geography and diverse management requirements will prove to be challenging.

Another factor is material sourcing. As materials become scarce (and more expensive) from traditional sources, cheaper sources will be sought. Additionally, new products and technologies will demand that new sources of materials (lithium salt deposits, for example) be found and commercialized. Both of these situations will require firms to adjust their logistical and environmental practices in order to meet the demands of shifting geographic locations and increasingly strict sustainability standards (those imposed by legislation and those imposed by social activism).

A third factor is the informational requirements that are being demanded across the supply chain. More data is being required for inventory visibility, sourcing verification, and environmental impact—just to name a few. Firms are collecting and analyzing consumption and consumer data with increased volume and speed, to develop insights that can impact supply-chain resource deployment, supply-chain design, and supply-sustainability activities.

Most of the world's population is classified as developing economically, or not in a "rich" country with well-developed formal supply chains. Firms need to better understand how consumers at the bottom of the pyramid move and access products so they can afford them. Some of these supply chains include illegal or illegitimate networks that siphon off significant resources from businesses, but some are full of innovation that allow folks to obtain what they want and need. Businesses need to figure out how to tap into this knowledge in order to develop supply-chain capability and services for the bottom of the pyramid, and provide products to customers at the extremes or in areas that do not have fully developed or traditional infrastructure networks.

Unfortunately, **low-end workers are increasingly being devalued and viewed as expendable.** These workers perform the essential tasks needed to support business operations. Their roles can be based in agriculture or manufacturing, be part of the logistical efforts to move goods through our resource networks, or provide the customer facing services required to keep retail stores, hospitals, and restaurants open to serve customers. Many organizations take the people that pick our fruit, deliver our packages, and clean our hotel rooms for granted (as evidenced by their treatment during the COVID-19 pandemic) or do not view (or treat them) as a key part of the firm's ability to serve customers or deliver value to stakeholders along the supply chain. But we can, and must, do better.

The Future of Talent for Supply-Chain Jobs

Labor supply chains are often overlooked and typically thought of merely as ways to get the people needed to complete the tasks associated with manufacturing or delivering products for customers.

One gap in the labor supply chain is that **diversity of both thought and presence is lacking in many leadership areas of supply-chain management**. There are plenty of people of color working in the labor roles (trucking, pick/pack, manufacturing, distribution/warehouses, etc.) and even in the roles that supervise them (team lead, supervisors, etc.). But there is often no path from the distribution centers or plants to organizational leadership, so most of these employees and supervisors will be perpetually relegated to lower-level roles. Even as more firms are recognizing the need for more diversity in the overall leadership within the higher levels of an organization, they often continue to neglect the need for, and benefits of, developing a workforce and leadership ranks that reflect the diversity of the markets and sources that make up the network. This gap puts supply-chain related functions at a disadvantage when competing for leadership talent.

Compounding the diversity gap, universities are lacking in their ability to train future supply chain talent. **Students need to have more instruction about the world of highly interconnected resource** networks.

As both an company marketing professional as well as a business school professor, I realize that my classroom is a key source for some of the labor and leadership of the firms that my students will populate, and the resource networks that they will lead in the future. The type of training many students are getting is not necessarily best suited for them to think broadly about solving daily operational business problems. They are also not learning to develop innovative ways to cope with the changing dynamics of an increasingly smaller, more volatile, and more interconnected planet. It is not the specific classes or subject matter that I believe is problematic, but rather the type of learning.

To better prepare for the world of highly-interconnected resource networks, not every business student needs to major in supply-chain management, but there needs to be more exposure to how supply chains and resource networks support our business systems. This type of learning is different from the operations management (OM) training that is part of the core curriculum at most business schools. OM classes focus on how to efficiently manage facilities to meet economic objectives. Future business leaders also need to understand how to manage the disruptions, evolving risks, and altered logistics that that are making our world more turbulent, particularly after the COVID-19 pandemic.

In this new era, many potential students have become comfortable with remote learning. Additional infrastructure is needed to increase the capability of business schools to educate students in formats that better match the reality of student's lives. Top schools are leaning into delivering instruction to students in a variety of formats (in-person, online asynchronously, or online synchronously) while mid-tier (and lower) schools are struggling to differentiate themselves. There is competition from for-profit online schools for students that are struggling to decide between online education and traditional face-to face schools. These students are working, may have families, or are non-traditional and are not looking for the traditional four-year, on-campus experience. Schools must have ways for these students to get the education they desire.

Additionally, students need a clearer understanding of how their skills and knowledge acquired from college will fit into the work structures of today's corporations. I am observing that they have no real idea of how much they are worth (what salaries should be) or how to go about finding a place to work and begin developing marketable skills.

Business schools should also help students understand the **investment** of education. It seems that college has become a rite-of-passage that many embark upon in hopes of delaying "adulting" and/or as a placeholder until they "find themselves." Career planning and post-college strategy seem to be more and more scarce, resulting in graduates having more debt, fewer sustainable opportunities, and a growing sentiment that college is no longer "worth it."

The perception that college is the only path for a prosperous middle-class life has pushed more people to seek higher education. This increased competition means more students will not be admitted to a top-tier program. For a variety of reasons, more students are attending smaller, less expensive schools that do not get the same resources or have access to the same business networks that students at top schools have access to. This lack of access can result in students graduating without the exposure or skills employers are looking for, putting these students behind their peers and limiting the types of opportunities made available to them.

Next Steps: How do we Mitigate Some of These Challenges?

The turbulence and change that our resource networks are soon to experience will be challenging. Many firms will not prepare until it is too late, and those firms will falter. Firms that intend to survive should take some of the following actions to mitigate the new problems and old thinking that can make future survival difficult. This will require firms to think differently about their supply chains, and educators to think differently about their students. Our next steps should be to address interconnected resource network challenges by looking at how businesses design, manage, and develop their resource networks, including talent.

Think about How Supply Chains are Designed

Firms must re-think how their resource networks are designed. Efficiency and cost will always be a consideration, but future supply chains must:

Redesign for Risk and Disruption

For supply chains, the interruption of planned flows of man, materials, money, or information will cause problems. The uncertainty introduced can cause network members to behave in more self-interested ways (such as stockpiling resources or restricting distribution), which can impact weaker supply chains and have a cascade effect, spreading the disruption farther, faster.

Our desire for efficient and lean supply chains, coupled with levels of increasing integration and interconnectedness across the world, introduces a new degree of risk that is not fully understood because a) many firms only think about the parts of their supply chain that are in their sphere of influence/control, and b) supply chains are only noticed when there is a problem (cost, quality, product availability, etc.).

Firms are too often unaware of potential issues that can disrupt supply chains or hamper resiliency. A labor dispute at a major port, or a typhoon in a remote region of the world, can impact global manufacturing systems because we've designed a system with limited suppliers and little room for uncertainty. Political disputes, weather (climate change), and unpredictable crises like global pandemics should be considered when determining how your resource network will look.

Redesign for New Logistics
Supply-chain designers of the future will have to reevaluate some long-held mindsets because the factors that helped shape prior strategic thinking have shifted. Cost and quality will no longer be the leading factors that drive network design decisions; other factors will need to be considered. More re-shoring and near-shoring must occur to help networks become more resilient and reduce product availability issues. New risk profiles in networks will need to be developed due to impacts from climate change, such as low rainfall in Panama, for example, that changes transit characteristics of the Panama Canal. Political changes impact international boundaries, treaties, and access to markets, which affect the risk profiles of supply network designs. Technological changes introduce new logistical capabilities powered by artificial intelligence, data availability, and new manufacturing methods. 3D printing, for example, will change where products

are made and how they are delivered, changing the resource networks for items ranging from automobiles to new homes. Increased automation and new materials handling technology will be part of the new designs—autonomous vehicles in closed systems and drones will improve throughput, increase efficiency, expand reach, and reduce costs of doing business. Application of technology for materials handling will do the same (e.g., Google Glass, augmented reality, blockchain, etc.).

More cross-functional integration will also be required in new network designs. In my experience, three other fields must be included when designing world-class supply chains for the future: marketing, information technology, and finance. The connection between these fields for developing the products that customers value and want is important, but the ability to *deliver* those products in a way that is cost effective and provides a *customer experience* that reflects the company's brand is just as important, if not more so.

The immense amount of data that is generated by customers/consumers can inform many parts of the business. IT provides marketing insights to understanding customers and trends for future developments. For supply chain, IT provides valuable data on performance, asset utilization (inventory visibility, inventory deployment, etc.), and demand pattern that can be used to manage risk and supplement the decisions of the sales and marketing group. Because Supply Chain Management and Logistics (SCM/L) is viewed as a cost center in many organizations, it is important to understand how the performance and efficiency of supply networks impact the bottom line. These connections, and ensuring customer experiences are in line with brand promises for the B2B and B2C customers, will become increasingly important as supply chains become more consumer-centric.

Redesign for More Consumer/Customer Centricity

As mentioned above, marketing, finance, logistics, and customer data will need to be more tightly connected in future supply-chain designs. The concept of Consumer-Centric Supply Chain Management[9] will be part of future supply-chain design as firms work to include consumer desires and experiences into their value-delivery networks. Recycling activities, fair-trade principles, and humane farming practices are examples of solutions and experiences consumers value and will pay a premium for, made possible through supply chain design and capability.

As supply chains become more critical to firm success, we will increasingly see firms try to skim the most profitable customers, which can leave poorer (typically minority and low-income) communities with lower levels of access to mainstream networks. This logistics redlining could take the form of limited transportation, inequitable food distribution/access, sub-par delivery resources, and lower levels of the distribution of information-based products. As consumer-centric supply chains are developed, firms will need to account for all levels of consumers and the diverse markets in which they exist.

Marketing communications and advertising is still important, but future supply-chain designers must realize that customer value is not just the functional utility of days past. It incorporates form, time, and place utility as well. Being able to communicate that you understand the total picture of your value proposition and can deliver what businesses and consumers value is important. Designing the capability to deliver what customers value will require that firms evaluate their ability to engage in last-mile logistics. This is more than just dropping off packages. Last-mile logistics is the final and sometimes only engagement a customer has with a firm outside of the (internet) ordering process. Not only does this put customer engagement in the hands of a part of the organization that is not typically exposed to or trained in customer engagement, but many firms outsource this work to other organizations such as Amazon or the USPS.

Redesign for Better Use of Resources

Sustainability is critical when redesigning future resource networks. The natural resources we use to feed our consuming world (and resource networks) are in limited supply. This is due to the absolute amounts that exist, time-driven replenishment or generation cycles, or cost. Redesigning resource networks will require that organizations be more aware of their supply chain composition and demand that fellow network members provide their products in responsible ways.

This becomes even more of a problem as firms outsource more parts of their supply chain. By using third-party providers, firms are becoming more removed from the first-hand knowledge of how the resource networks they rely on are being run. Environmentally unfriendly farming, aquaculture, and mining practices are tolerated because they can result in lower cost supply, particularly when sourcing from developing parts of the world.

New designs must make it unacceptable for firms to ignore the negative practices of other members of their resource networks. Regulation, legislation, and corporate peer-pressure are some ways to eliminate suppliers that use methods or practices that jeopardize ecological systems, their local communities, or customer reputations. Leveraging new tracking technologies, chain-of custody protocols, and reporting procedures can help expose poor actors that must be rooted out and removed from the network. Businesses must not forget that consumers and investors will increasingly hold them accountable for the outcomes of their supply chains, including the behavior of their suppliers.

Human and labor resources must be managed responsibly as well. Some firms prioritize efficiency and cost without sufficient concern for the people (labor), or for the means by which raw materials are acquired to meet supply chain goals. Labor is a huge cost component, so some firms take advantage of workers via low wages and poor working conditions.

New designs must have built-in mechanisms to safeguard against worker exploitation, and expose network members that produce or accept products produced with such labor.

Development of human capital will be different in a post-COVID world—how people work, learn, and engage will involve more remoteness and more technology. Firms must intentionally incorporate life-long learning concepts into their HR management, while preparing for the fact that digital natives will soon become the bulk of the workforce, and technology competence will be required for an effective workforce.

Firms (and society) must understand that there will be a shift from the binary choice of college-bound vs. not college-bound. Educational institutions (high school and colleges) and firms must allow and help create alternative pathways for future workers to gain education and skills which can be converted into income more quickly and in ways that support non-traditional students[10]. The "upskilling" program Amazon uses is an example of such work, where it enables workers to become more skilled in ways that the firm values and can result in higher incomes,[11],[12]. This means changes to knowledge delivery systems (more use of technology to deliver content, more options/flexibility to receive content) and changes to what is presented as an acceptable or valuable career (skilled trades, etc.)

Think about How Supply Chains are Managed
Internally, many firms have supply-chain challenges with respect to how the different functions relate to each other. Whether balancing cost reduction in the supply chain, the risk of supply disruption, or marketing objectives, there often seems to be an internal disconnect across key departments and between their functions that encourages each to maximize itself vs. optimize the entire business. This can lead to persistently sub-optimized systems.

This disconnect across the marketing/supply chain interface often happens because the marketing (commercial) function in many businesses is at odds with, or uneducated about, their supply chain. In some of the companies where I have worked, the supply chain/operations part of the company is separate from the commercial side of the business. Although projects that require supply-chain involvement are discussed and worked out, true integration of these two parts of the business is less common.

When these functions are not integrated, incentives can become misaligned. To correct this, firms must treat marketing and supply-chain management (commercial and operational functions of the business) as allies in creating and delivering value to customers, not adversaries that fight for corporate dollars at each other's expense. For some organizations, sales and marketing should have some accountability for inventory levels because they help determine customer order patterns and order sizes. Likewise, manufacturing and logistics should have some accountability for customer satisfaction, because this function influences the experience of customers via delivery and quality of performance. Both groups should share proportionally in rewards or penalties. The exact metrics will change from company to company, but the goal should be that overall organizational success is dependent on an optimal system, and the metrics used to manage organizational behavior should reflect that goal.

By increasing the interaction of the two groups, more value could be delivered to customers as the marketing group works with the supply chain to develop value-added services or other customer-pleasing offerings that are supply chain driven rather than purely R&D or product development driven. Innovative delivery solutions, developing unique manufacturing processes, and integrated supply teams are examples of ways firms can use their supply chain expertise to provide additional value to customers.

External behaviors of firms will also need to be adjusted. Large organizations will need to do a better job at balancing their responsibility to shareholders with their responsibility to the public good. Governments are increasingly looking to the private sector for help with supporting social issues and providing social safety nets. The corporate social responsibility messaging that is frequently used as a marketing tactic to improve brand equity with consumers must be more than talking points. Companies that have become cultural institutions will need to use their power for the greater good, not just shareholder value. This can come in the form of better sourcing practices, higher prices paid to third-world sources of agricultural supply, or more environmentally sustainable manufacturing methods.

Companies such as Starbucks make investments in their networks by supporting dairy suppliers to develop more sustainable production methods[13], and working with coffee farmers to introduce technological and agricultural advancements to improve sustainability and farmer profitability[14]. Inditex, a global, multi-branded fashion company, has also invested in its supply chain to improve transparency, traceability, and working conditions of its labor force[15]. These are just two examples that reflect how firms are beginning to understand how their sourcing practices have impact across the globe, and are changing their behavior to more positively impact the broad range of stakeholders they impact.

More work needs to be done to help small businesses improve their resource network capabilities. Many of the prominent technology-oriented solutions are too complex or too costly for small businesses to implement. Small firms may not have the knowledge or capital resources required to take advantage of the efficiencies or other benefits of enhanced supply-chain capabilities, leaving them at a disadvantage. These smaller businesses at the "bottom of the supply chain" would benefit from training on supply-chain fundamentals such as inventory management, strategic sourcing, continuous improvement strategies, and technology integration. This would result in stronger, more resilient links in the resource network.

Think about the Talent (People) Pipeline

People provide the labor to make garments, harvest agricultural products, pick packages in warehouses, and run the technologies that enable production. People are a critical part of the global resource networks that businesses use to supply themselves. Investing in people is a key area that must be addressed to mitigate supply-chain challenges and ensure that more innovation, knowledge resources, and highly capable workers are available to network members in the future.

Internally to firms, the investment to improve opportunities can come in many forms. One way is to ensure there are opportunities for workers to have professional development pathways to continually improve their economic and knowledge potential. As mentioned previously, many of the people in the supply-chain workforce (warehouse workers, assemblers, inventory specialists, etc.) and their supervisors are relegated to lower-level roles, and typically have no pathways to rise to corporate leadership or other higher-paying jobs. Reskilling and upskilling programs will help provide the additional knowledge needed for career growth. Career roadmaps will help employees have more vision for how to develop their own careers. All this will improve retention of workers and, critically, the institutional knowledge they possess.

New knowledge and institutional knowledge are important for supply-chain success, and new thinking must cultivate both. Individual firms can address educational challenges in resource networks by introducing more continual/lifelong learning into their workforces. The speed of change and innovation in the marketplace does not allow current workers to rest on their laurels, to cherry-pick who will develop new skills and knowledge, or wait until crisis mode before being forced to improve, update, or enhance their skills.

Companies will also have to invest in improving working conditions across their supply chains to attract and retain talent. This includes working hours/patterns and future opportunities in the firm (promotability), in the supply chain and perhaps also in other applicable areas. Firms should take appropriate steps to make sure the supply chain is viewed as a fun, engaging, important part of the business, not just a job in a warehouse. Just as the commercial or financial parts of the business market themselves as career destinations, the SCM/L of the business must do the same.

Externally to the firm, supply networks must invest in supporting opportunities for the workers and businesses that feed the networks. This support can come from enforcement of workers' rights rules, paying fair prices to small farmers for agricultural products, micro-loans to small entrepreneurs in developing countries, or partnering with suppliers to train them in the latest quality management protocols. These types of investments will strengthen each link in the supply chain, making it more resilient and able to quickly adjust to ever-changing global forces.

Direct efforts must be made to better connect industry and academia. Research produced by academics is not perceived as useful to most practitioners. The reality is, academics research and report on many aspects of supply-chain topics in efforts to develop theoretical insights about the relationships between a multitude of factors that can influence performance and other business outcomes. But a good portion of it is developed and communicated in a way that does not speak to its practical value for firms.

Practitioners sometimes criticize academics for being in the "Ivory Tower," but it is sometimes difficult for academics to get access to the shop floor. Addressing this challenge requires that academics develop better connections to real-world business firms. These connections can take the form of internships for students and professors, classroom participation by practitioners, or councils that keep educational teams informed about skills, trends, and topics relevant to supply chain employers. Maintaining these connections is important in that the people who are doing research in the field, training future practitioners, and developing the "latest thinking" will have access to the most current class materials, subject matter, and topics that are valuable to the progress and development of firms.

Although typically outside of their purview, firms will need to take a greater role in assisting colleges and universities with training students (future employees) and exposing them to some of the social aspects of participating in the corporate workforce and certain sectors of American society—particularly for those who may have diverse backgrounds or may be classified as non-traditional students. Cohort programs that allow students to come together and develop communities to embrace their new environment and opportunities can be a way to enhance the college experience and support retention. Mentorship is another way to help provide students with coaching and support for social challenges encountered during the college experience. An enhancement to this type of support would be some form of training on how to cultivate the mentor/protégé relationship. Many mentors have backgrounds in common that helped them develop the wisdom and experience to be a mentor. Protégés, on the other hand, have little to no knowledge/exposure to fully understand the opportunities being presented, and could benefit from systematically learning how to be better fertile ground for the opportunities that come with having a mentor. This would support a more productive experience.

Supply-chain owners must recognize the need to compete for talent. World-class supply chains will require deliberate efforts to develop and promote world-class, diverse talent. Firms have learned how to attract/recruit diverse talent and bring them into the corporate structure, but still struggle to provide pathways for them to rise through the corporate ranks. Although top leadership understands the need for the development of talent, they have been unable to implement change amongst their management ranks (the gatekeepers) so that diverse talent can get the opportunity to lead others, get experience in the business, or get exposure to the required networks that lead to promotion and success. This behavior persists despite various industry reports and research indicating that diverse leadership improves firm performance and employee satisfaction.

Summary

In the near future, our world will become more turbulent and change in ways that we cannot predict. Our societies will continue to demand consumer products, and businesses will find ways to provide them. This cycle of demand and supply drives international trade and fuels economies all over the world. Developing resource networks have been the catalysts for some of humanity's greatest adventures, and the reasoning behind some of its greatest atrocities. My overall goal with this chapter was to remind you how interconnected our supply networks are, as well as their role in keeping the world stable. I also wanted to provide some perspective on thought processes I have seen that, if not changed, will introduce risk and vulnerability into these critical systems.

Whether you are a seasoned supply-chain professional or new to the issues and concepts presented above, I hope you agree that we must have innovative ideas that change how we design, develop, and manage these networks. Some ideas will be controversial because they question the status quo with respect to profit motives and accountability for the actions of suppliers. Other ideas will be difficult to implement because they will change the calculus for determining the value of supply sources. When impacts on the environment, local communities, and potentially customers are taken into account, we may make different decisions on how and where to source products.

Proactively addressing these issues in our future supply chains is one of the biggest challenges we will face, partially because society does not grasp how dependent it is upon resource exchange networks. Food, clothing, energy, medicine, you name it – they all require networks of supply. We only notice when these systems fail, and then we rush to repair them. Convincing current network owners they need to invest in a changing future will be difficult without the specter of the loss of profit, or even outright failure, hanging over them.

Reader, you must be courageous by consistently inserting mitigations into the networks you influence. Many firms with large supply requirements have reams of procedures and protocols for suppliers. Do you know which suppliers are compliant? What about your 2nd or 3rd tier suppliers? Is anyone watching them? What actions do you take to engage with partner functions in your firm? How is your supply chain capability being developed to be more consumer centric?

These are just a few examples of many questions that can be asked, and their answers can help put firms on a path towards better management of our supply chains.

Chapter Seven

What Robin Hood Tells Us About Confronting the Climate Crisis (and Other World Trends)

By Bruce Piasecki

"It is not what you say, it is what they hear!"

This insight is one of the key discoveries of the last century. From marketing strategies to neuroscience research, we have discovered that what we communicate is not just received on its basic facts.

A good story, a tale, is absorbed through the human psyche and experience. The impact of its message is just as much felt as understood. Thus, when trying to steer people toward change, how we communicate with each other is as important as what we communicate.

Making a Difference in Our Lives through Words and Deeds

Why does this matter?

I believe we're approaching a new era in which significant progress on climate change (and other social issues) can be made. Since the 2007 financial crisis, the disruptive promise of the environmental, social, and governance movement has taken hold in the business world. This ESG momentum has, like a surging river, joined with the women's movement, the diversity and inclusion movement, and the sustainability movement to make a torrent of practical changes.

Some vivid results include the passing of the Inflation Reduction Act, which includes over $400 billion in climate solution technologies and subsidies. Another is the CHIPS innovation grants. These two recent Titan-like giant steps will help many to get off the petrochemical treadmill. Big oil was a thing of 120 years ago, these movements suggest, and by osmosis, the new generation of consumers and thinkers expect change, not entrenched positions of power and limited purpose.

The Shortfall That Remains Involves Redistribution

But while these big-step changes have begun to happen in investment markets, national policies, and global corporations, they have not yet been widely recognized or embraced by the general public. You see this in the climate change opinion polls organized across the last 15 years by groups at Yale, George Mason, and Stanford.

This is not to say that people aren't ready for solutions on our climate crisis. After reviewing the historic trends, I believe the majority of humans across 192 nations are now ready for serious action on climate change. But while attitude and urgency indicators have changed, confusion on action paths remains.

A Reason to Rethink Your Life as a Robin Hood with Your Friends as Merry Pranksters

It is becoming clear that action paths will require some rebalancing of resources and responsibility between the wealth and commonwealth in our society. My new book *Wealth and Climate Competitiveness* outlines a new narrative with examples from firms as different as Trane Technologies, bp, and six others.

Yet, disabling prejudices against such approaches remain in the popular imagination, based on damaging remnants from the past. This causes an overall cynicism toward the promise of carbon competitiveness and climate solutions. What can break apart those prejudices, and the limiting cynicism? We find it in recovering lasting tales.

To move forward, we need a new narrative to communicate solutions. One of the most effective ways we communicate with each other, and move our society forward, is through stories and fables that endure. Real change on the climate crisis will require a shared story we work from together, a story of what it takes to succeed by doing more with less. What is that shared story that can unite the torrents, the separate movements, into a cohesive force?

Luckily, we have an example right in front of us. For what story embodies these ideas of apt innovation, cleverness, and redistribution through friendship and community better than the tale of Robin Hood?

FIRST, A WARNING

Before we delve into Robin Hood, a word about the very essence of story and myth. Folk tales can be disruptive, even when people first see them as entertainment. This is because the narrative elements resonate emotionally.

A fable's depth resides in the collective psyche and in your mindful emotions. A good effective tale makes you think in a more inclusive way, about your family, your friends, and your firm. It is rapidly shared across different age groups and social levels.

Through the ages, we remember Robin Hood—and other tales of social advocates like those of Nelson Mandela and Desmond Tutu—for solid social reasons. When we experience, as readers, tales like those of Robin Hood, something happens throughout our brain. The response is not simply rational. We embrace the entertainment punch of the fable with an open heart and a more open mind, freeing ourselves of pre-judgment. The response, the neuroscientists show us, is similar to our enjoyment of music. Tales and music stimulate action in many parts of our brain, not just the language functions.

These tales, from any culture, get us past our simple prejudices into a realm of the collective socialized self—the commonwealth.

Robin Hood through the Years

Let's now take a closer look at the Robin Hood story. C. Holt offers, in a wonderful Folio Society edition, the most comprehensive account of the legend of Robin Hood. It pays to itemize some of the historic lessons from this legend, as we consider it for our era.

1. Robin Hood, as a name in England, appeared as early as 1296, over 700 years ago, around the time Dante was writing about business and society in Italia. Both Dante's *Divine Comedy* and the stories about Robin Hood are classics in exploring business and society and wealth within the commonwealth, when you read them properly as lasting cultural fables.
2. Holt explains how this tale about wealth, justice, and injustice led to the creation of Robin Hood mimics in the popular May festivals.

There is plenty of evidence about church festivities celebrating Robin Hood.

3. Holt wants us to understand that his book is about a legend rather than a man. He asserts: *"The identity of the man matters less than the persistence of the legend. That is the most remarkable thing about him."* This makes me think of the how the stories of figures like Gandhi and George Floyd have developed into something larger than life.

4. Holt explains how the legend *"snowballed, collecting fragments of other stories as it rolled along."* Even *"the central character was re-modelled. At his first appearance Robin was a yeoman. He was then turned into a nobleman unjustly deprived of his inheritance, later into an Englishman protecting his native countryman from the domination of the* Normans."

   These ideas of economic revenge evolved as the image of Robin Hood changed, even up to the 1960s when he became like a quintessential social rebel. His hair grew long, flowing in the winds.

5. Holt continues: *"At first sight the legend is about justice. Robin is at once an embodiment of honor and an agent of retribution. He corrects the evil which flows from the greed of rich clerics and the corruption of the royal* officials."

   Yet here is the key point for this book: *"But he does not seek to overturn social conventions. On the contrary, Robin Hood sustains these conventions against the machinations of the wicked and the powerful who explicitly flout and undermine them."*

Points one(1) through six(6) constitute, in my experience, the elements of the new narrative required to unite the momentum in the social movements, and to unite the generations.

I cannot place enough emphasis on the subtle appropriation significance in point five, that the tale "does not seek to overturn social conventions." That is its genius in melding solution paths between the dominant culture and its emerging and reactionary cultures. Think of it as the blending of the different types of cultures already at play in industrial societies, as it helps align the force within markets, technology, governments, the press, and your personal consumer behaviors.

What else do we need to embrace about the Robin Hood story? Throughout the centuries that the tale of Robin Hood has been told, and all its evolutions over time, a few key characteristics always remain the same:

1. Robin Hood keeps his word before his brethren, while the treacherous sheriff does not. He is portrayed as an emerging new man, while the clerics, the nobles, and the sheriff are fixed.
2. Robin Hood is always presented as doing more with less, as frugal, alert, and clever. In episode after episode, he is presented as nimbler than the indulgent clerics and administrators making a villain of him. I take this to mean that Robin Hood is not burdened with heavy baggage. Instead, he is light and capable of doing much more with less.
3. Most important, Robin Hood is a generous human being. He wins our hearts and minds by taking what is criminal and giving it back to the poor in a magical transformation of generosity. We do not think of him as a criminal, as we no longer think of Nelson Mandela as "criminal" or Henry David Thoreau as "subversive."

It is my belief that all who want to see progress in the coming years, especially climate-change advocates, must find a way to become a new Robin Hood in our culture. They must be seen just as trustworthy, frugal, and generous as our cultural hero.

Climate competitiveness engages these more positive forces in social change.

Again, this happens in the new narrative without revolution or social chaos. In fact, the opposite happens. Societies across the nations re-achieve the lost balance between business and society, between wealth and the commonwealth, in ways that redistribute wealth to those that are climate competitive.

By examining a tale like Robin Hood through the ages, we suggest that a higher truth needs to be embraced the rest of this century: frugality requires a kind of militancy. The arts of competitive frugality—the entirety of the ESG movements—constitute, through billions of investment clicks, a kind of "stealing from the rich to give to the poor." These investment militants are like Robin Hood, as they are embarrassing the wasteful and the leisurely to take climate change seriously through tens of thousands of clicks per trading day, globally.

Good Trouble

In the end, the tale of Robin Hood is a tale of defiance. The balance of what is good for the commonwealth and what is bad behavior of the wealthy changes over time. Overall, the intolerance of idle waste has increased through this century. The world is ready for a Robin Hood mentality again. And it begins with each new person "getting the tale's impact."

It is my hope that this chapter will put you in this shared frame of mind. The age of climate and capital constraints requires no less. "Doing more with less" is the mantra of this century's success stories.

World Trends and the Next Forms of Advanced Capitalism

When I first met Darryl Vernon Poole, it was related to my 2007 book *World Inc.* going global at the time. Darryl had honored me by coming to my National Press Club talk on that book, and then shared its essence in his newsletters and alerts many times. I assumed he liked how it summed up globalization, both from its upsides and its downward features.

What follows is my summary of what has been made true in global trends since 2007, for your use as a "message in a bottle" for the future.

Advancing Capitalism Today and Tomorrow

The world of this new century, so swift and severe, needs superior leadership, as described in the prior chapters of this collection. As in the two prior centuries, competing on price and quality remain critical and necessary. That is the prevailing essence of capitalism, industry, and governments in the free world. But today, these two fountainheads of capitalism are providing insufficient criteria for success in a carbon- and capital-constrained world.

What else is needed? We heard parts of these answers in the work provided by Keith Story on supply-chain improvements, by Dennis Easter on using information platforms, and by Larry Clay on filling in better educational gaps. My essay works to provide the glue to bind these global trends working to improve the world.

I believe we need something no less than a new kind of leader. Most social commentators today, from Lt Colonel Phillips to Darryl Vernon Poole, note that we need leaders we can trust, leaders who can compete on price, quality and social needs—from avian and swine flu or the COVID Pandemic, to new forms of energy, and better cars, computers and homes.

How do we get to these kinds of competencies? First off, as suggested in the works by Larry Clay, we need to combine the best that MBAs get with what Masters of Public Administration know and experience. How is this possible? And where will they work?

I believe we need something no less than a new kind of leader, and an advanced form of capitalism…what I call Social Response Capitalism.

Defining Social Response Capitalism

My definition of the burgeoning form of advanced capitalism is not without complexity and consequences. Here are some of the tenets of Social Response Capitalism:

1. Companies restructure their operations to actively accommodate consumer demand by creating new products that bridge the gap between traditional expectations of performance and price and social impact on the larger world.

2. This gap has been ignored in the past because it wasn't considered good business to worry about such "externalities."

3. However, today, these externalities are impinging upon the long-term viability of entire product lines that have served as the basis for our industrial economy.

4. While past efforts at becoming a good corporate citizen often focused on streamlining production techniques and efficiency, the latest twist is making better products—products that respond to legitimate, emerging social pressures and needs.

Examples of these new social pressures include a drive to eliminate toxic chemicals in products of everyday use, a new corporate emphasis on the reusability and endurance of products, and some early examples of pure product innovation in advance response to pressures on clean air and climate change. Since *World, Inc.* was published, I've concentrated on applying the tenets to climate competitiveness, as seen above in the narrative of Robin Hood.

The Larger Social Context of Altruism, Capitalism, and Social Response

Altruism requires evidence of selfless good; social response simply requires not shooting those on your side. It means you create a web of support within your firm, industry, and the regulatory community. You basically recreate the rules on what determines a "good" product—addressing public expectations in a sensible and reliable business fashion—thus ensuring that you are able to compete on price, technical quality, and social needs. This is especially true for firms providing security, sensors, energy, cars, and computers.

This kind of "Business for Good" was first articulated by CEO Bill Novelle in his classic *Good Business*. Since writing this book, Mr. Novelli has become a strong proponent of my leader-to-leader workshops known as the Corporate Affiliates Achieving Results Workshops. There are now 3,000 executives who have engaged us in this type of capitalism, and I am sure there are tens of thousands more who we have not yet had the chance to meet.

I now believe this force for good is increasingly evident among capitalists across the world. These capitalists understand altruism, and are doing more and better by applying these social principles and needs in their competitive organizations.

Three Key Challenge Areas: The "S Frontier"

In the 21st century, three key elements will challenge businesses: I call it the "S Frontier. " The S Frontier is comprised of: the swiftness of information, the severity of global problems, and the need for business leaders to become "social response capitalists."

You can find the full details about this concept in my original *World, Inc.* book. For now, please know that this S Frontier touches all firms, from large, responsible companies such as Electrolux and Whirlpool to small firms looking for their niche and barriers against competition.

Once you know to look for it, the trained eye sees it almost everywhere, and realizes that the day of the cheap, shoddy product is coming to an end. Nike sees this, as do Starbucks, IBM, Patagonia, and Unilever. In fact, if you study the top 17 "recognized leading firms" in the empirical studies published by Chris Coulter, you'll see these Social Response Principles in action.

It is about building to a new, higher peak from which to compete on price, technical quality, and social response. These corporations are seeing that more and more people are refusing to buy goods that don't meet a certain standard, even if they are cheaper.

This revolution in quality, efficient manufacturing have established the dual corporate emphasis on price and the technical quality of products and organizations.

Firms like GE, Honeywell, Lockheed Martin, and ConocoPhillips are now famous for employing this dual emphasis on price and technical quality to bring better products into the world. Yet there is so much more at play now in the world, as Larry Clay, Keith Story, and others note in this book.

A New Trinity of Social and Corporate Beliefs

We now live in a time of a new corporate trinity, a set of beliefs that puts social concerns on par with price and performance.

This new approach to business strategy is designed to promote "sustained value creation." It produces families of products that can stand up to social scrutiny over time. To the ever-present pursuit of lowering price while improving technical quality, Social Response Product Development introduces a new decision model.

As a result, companies are taking on unfamiliar new roles that can build the long-term value of their business and fundamentally change the quality of our everyday lives. If price and technical quality are the "father" and the "son" of this corporate creed, then Social Response is the "holy ghost" for many companies.

To date, this third part of the trinity has been largely invisible. This anthology assembles actual industrial practices to illustrate it more visibly.

The truth is that the social mission of a firm is becoming more firmly embedded in everything they do, as consumers and competitors keep raising the bar on socially responsible products. That is why writers such as Scott Bedbury, the creator of the earthy yet sassy feel of corporate brands like Nike and Starbucks, have so much fun talking about the "soul" of an organization. When a firm asks questions about how the future needs of society will reshape their organization, then you begin to feel their soul.

Give Them What They Need, Not Just What They Want

Social Response Capitalism is rapidly growing in importance in all corners of the global marketplace. It is grabbing center stage in select corporate boardrooms throughout the world. My experience with firms like HP and DuPont dictates that this is not a passing fad. The CEOs may leave, but this kind of culture will remain. The need to compete on price, technical quality, and social response has historical underpinning and economic success tied to it now. It is constantly updated and modified, but ever-present and permanent.

What's Surprising and What's New About Social Leadership

The development of, and call for, social responsibility is quite new. This phenomenon is so new, in fact, that you really can't blame Deming and Juran for not noticing this emerging trend in their time. Indeed, most of the well-published management gurus of today (from Warren Bennis to Jim Collins) are still so preoccupied with the duality of price and quality that their very good work suffers from the lack of this promising third variable to success.

However, a few pioneering corporations are trailblazing ahead, changing faster than the ideas being espoused in traditional circles of scholarship and theory. Starbucks, Nike, Shell, and bp have spent millions on advertising to promote their "social brands." In a similar manner to what Deming and Juran did for corporate strategy after World War II, many new social forces began to alter the standard decision models of corporate strategy after the tragic accidents of Bhopal and the Exxon Valdez oil spill.

After working for Mario Cuomo and expanding my definition of the legitimate roles of government, I chronicled this trend in my 1995 book *Corporate Environmental Strategy: The Avalanche of Change since Bhopal*. I was thankful when Andy Hoffman, within two years, wrote a book called *Competitive Environmental Strategy* that echoed many of the same themes in a larger organizational dynamic context. Last but not least, Elsevier Science soon began publishing the quarterly *The Journal of Corporate Environmental* Strategy.

But what I failed to notice in all of these developments at the time was the sheer speed and magnitude of these changes.

Social Response Capitalism is much larger now than when I wrote *World, Inc.*, mostly because of changes within technologies, corporate strategy, and investment communities due to climate change. You can now witness this firsthand in how the internet reflects these concerns and interests. It resides, too, in consumer product selection, corporate strategy, investment appeal, and public brand. In my new 2024 books, I reflect on these spurts in new forms of capitalism explicitly.

Environmental Leadership, Climate Competitiveness, and Management Of Financial Risk And Opportunity

The ESG investment movement is difficult to snapshot, since it is like Robin Hood working each day in ten thousand clicks of the investors. Yet, it involves the entire search for superior products to secure a better world. It also drives discussion of a far broader range of topics within the world's major companies, which is both the result of Social Response Capitalism and the beginning of it.

The additional issues being addressed range from labor conditions in the factories located throughout Asia—a real concern of companies like Nike and Gap—to public health concerns. After the recent spate of natural disasters, fundamental lifesaving services—such as a clean and adequate water supply—are considered in this mix, along with modernizing the power grid. These developments will take decades to mature, at which point they will enter the mainstream lexicon of the press and the university.

As governments across the globe retreat on these issues, companies are increasingly expected to fill the void. When a firm asks questions about how the future needs of society will reshape their organization, then you begin to feel their soul.

Here is my point: history itself, like a giant advancing elephant, has changed capitalism, not just investors and governments.

Factors to Consider in Shaping Social Response Capitalism for the Future

The world now collectively faces some of the most serious threats to our normative sense of life, liberty, and enjoyment than ever before. The interconnections between global economic development, resource tension over oil and water, population growth, uncertainty over climate change, terrorism, and political unrest are all converging.

These catalysts are shaping the promising new developments in our global equity culture. The best social capitalists see the opportunity beneath these serious social challenges. Consider some of the following challenges to our current lifestyles in the coming decade:

1. **The world's population currently exceeds eight billion people**, placing large constraints on the capacity of the earth to provide for everyone.

2. **The majority of the world's population remains hungry, illiterate, and poor.**

3. **Butting up against constrained markets, many companies are extending their social responsibility reach into the poorest regions of the world** in hopes of helping them and one day creating a market for their products where one did not previously exist.

4. **The world's oil reserves are dwindling**; OPEC announced their expectation that oil will peak in 2035. Although some experts expect oil reserves to be depleted within fifty to one hundred years, I am of the school that believes social forces will intervene much sooner to prevent that further escalation of climate change.

5. **Energy is at the crux of sustainability.** More and more new technologies, policies, and investments are shaping the energy industry—fuel

cells, biofuels, wind power generation, thin-film photovoltaic power supplies, and bridge technologies like hybrid gasoline-electric engines. These technologies represent our growing awareness of finite resources.

6. **The availability of clean and fresh water is limited.** Some experts believe the global conflicts of the future will be "resource wars" related to gaining access to fresh water, fertile soil, and other natural resources.

7. **Economic growth in China is expected to continue exponentially for the next ten to twenty years,** potentially making them the second largest GDP worldwide by 2030. China is developing its economy with sustainability in mind. In 2003 and 2004, China adopted guidelines for automobile emissions and renewable energy technologies that, in some cases, go beyond the requirements in other developed countries. And yet today, more than two decades later, China still over-relies on cheap coal for their electrical demands, as they push for EV stations with giants like bp.

These are the usual mixed messages of social history: it is a highly competitive landscape, what I call the daily battle between speculative capitalists and social response capitalists.

Most good MBA and junior executives' minds start to wander after you share the first three of these global realities, and this is what separates the leader from the manager—the ability to cope and respond to new pressure.

The Boundary Conditions That Gave Birth to Social Response Capitalists

Here are the boundary conditions whereby this set of forces is reshaping capitalism:

- The one hundred largest multinational corporations (MNCs) now control about 20% of global foreign assets.

- As much as 40 percent of world trade now occurs within MNCs.

- Of the one hundred biggest economies in the world, 51 are corporations. Only 49 are governments.

- The annual sales revenues of each of the six largest multinational corporations are exceeded by the GDPs of only 21 countries in the world.

These facts, and continued rapid global corporate growth, have collided to form our new global equity culture. The best social capitalists see that this collision offers both opportunity and hope beneath these serious social challenges.

Post-World War II trends show that when rapid money transfers and corporate global demand on the price and availability of oil (for example) collide, it has repercussions that revolutionize how people and profits interact.

You see this most vividly in the ways energy and environmental decisions impact the economy—such as national security.

Read any Warren Buffett investment report and consider how things of global consequence are actually linked regionally, and even affect our lives through the business issues Keith Story has us think through in his chapter.

It is a very difficult image to convey to those unwilling to hear more than what directly impacts their bottom line. Social Response Capitalists hear them loud and clear. Herein lies the hope: to profit in a sustained way, you must leverage your money, corporate resources, energy, and people in a fashion that answers mounting social needs

This is why I founded the AHC Group forty-five years ago on this motto: "Answering Public Expectations." We use this motto to remind ourselves how small we are in the larger turbulence of global social needs. It is not about short-term markets only, but increasingly about long-term societal needs and expectations. We are still responding to the above factors—in fact, they reshape us monthly.

The Six Recurrent Benefits Enjoyed by Social Response Capitalists

For Social Response Capitalists, product stewardship and the management of their product families directly embody new forces within capitalism. One good idea is often quickly and creatively applied to as many products as is suitable. In less than three years, Toyota transferred its basic innovation of consequence—fuel efficiency—to ten of their models, from the Highlander SUV, the Camry, and the Lexus to some emerging high-efficiency trucks. HP does the same as it patterns innovations across product families—the liquid crystal display is one well-known case in point.

The post-Maytag Whirlpool will have to begin this process to compete with Electrolux properly. And, according to the well-financed and often-read pages of *Fortune* and *Forbes*, GE and Wal-Mart are after this kind of innovation as well. *Wired* and *Fast Company* frequently fill pages with the names of midsize and smaller companies hoping to do the same, as do *Inc.* and *CFO* magazine.

From 1999 to 2001, many of the key meetings we were invited to attend at Toyota had to do with this rigorous alignment of product families. As soon as the Prius reached 3% of the firm's global market share in 2005, Toyota let the *New York Times* print a piece about the ten-model implementation strategy we had conceived in 1999. At last, my confidentiality constraints could be lifted, and the logic of these Social Response Product

Development benefits could be generalized to benefit some of the other companies I worked with.

For three subsequent decades now, I have been advising clients that Social Response Product Development offers six recurrent benefits that compound like interest in a bank. As you read these, measure them in reference to a decade, not a quarterly report:

1. **Margin improvement**—seeking cost savings at every stage of the product life cycle through more efficient use of labor, energy, and material resources. Toyota is world-famous for such lean manufacture.

2. **Rapid cycle time**—reducing the time it takes to get a product to market by considering environmental issues as part of the concurrent engineering process during the early stages of design. Intel, HP, GE, and Honeywell benchmark these advances frequently.

3. **Global market access**—developing global products that are environmentally preferable and meet international eco-labeling standards in Europe, Japan, and other important trade regions. In 2006, after a significant new Goldman Sachs report itemized market access constraints in oil and gas, this strategic factor grew in importance for all global manufacturers. Toyota was there by 1999.

4. **Product differentiation**--introducing distinctive environmental benefits such as energy efficiency or ease of disassembly to your products may sway a purchase decision. Toyota out-competes all the auto giants in this category year after year.

5. **Social bundling of value in products**—positioning a company's product line in a fashion whereby it becomes clear to consumers and investors that this firm thinks of their products as social expressions,

as a compromise and a hybrid between addressing a social need and making some money.

6. **Reducing the risk premium of the firm**—by selecting products that have Social Response built into them, the overall risk profile of the firm is reduced. Social Response Product Development is a blend of classical product development along with this new set of "social" elements. Up until this new century, elements of yield improvement and market positioning across industries were limited to the realms of engineering performance specs and production criteria. But lately, social response has been reaching the upper levels of the corporate mansion, from the head of marketing and sales (as in the Toyota case) to the heads of law, IT, energy procurement, and the like.

Mounting Social Pressures Begat More Capitalists Who Think This Way

Social Response Capitalism is about to become much more prominent than it currently is. That's why it matters now to investors, managers, executives, supply-chain strategists, banks, and our entire global equity culture. To some extent, it doesn't really matter as much as I had thought it did if the consumer even sees this holy ghost of "social response." To profit in a sustained way you must leverage your money, corporate resources, energy, and people in a fashion that answers mounting social needs.

This is where the work of John Elkington, Joel Makower, and the other advocates of the green consumer fall short. When Social Response Capitalism works best, it is embedded in the price of the product—and becomes the invisible hand closing the purchase. In an important way, all the literature from 1972 to present on the need for "green consumers" misses this grounding point. I believe Patricia Aburdene's books started noting this new reality about ten years ago, as did the works of Stu Hart and others.

Social Response Capitalists have created these larger expectations that make it more difficult for their competitors to jump through the same hoops. It is in this act of making better products for a better world that Social Response Capitalists develop leaders we can trust.

Chapter Eight

Finale: Advice and Cascading Links

D.V. Poole

The purpose of this concluding essay is to put in one place our observations about significant world trends in the six years since 2018.

According to all our trend analysis and publications, the year 2024 escalated the past five-year trend of globally painful transitions, missed policy opportunities, and profound human challenges. We chose these words carefully: it was a "a trend of globally **painful** transitions."

We say this with two operational observations: 1) our institutions have exhibited insensitivity and failures; yet, 2) our people have demonstrated extraordinary individual compassion, self-sacrifice, and continuous resiliency. You see this not only in the work of our chapter authors, but in the hundreds of thousands of others that their work "sums up," and shares here for you.

Many professionals, businesses, corporations, and practitioners are actively engaging their own comprehensive lists of trends and issues facing the world today and in the future. Though my observations may not be unique, they illustrate several commonalities in risk patterns:

- In many regions of the world, we are exhibiting early-stage volatile convergence, a cascading intensity of trends.
- Our experts suggest that these cascading convergences cannot be stopped through "traditional" legal, legislative, or PR efforts.
- Instead, any of the arks described by Robin Noel Phillips in her chapter require insight, relevance, intellectual honesty,

judgement, and cooperation to either moderate, mediate, mitigate, correct, and/or stop these cascading trends. You sense the same in the other contributors, and certainly, in the differing work of Piasecki and myself.

Since 2018, each of us has found ourselves asking: *"What really happened here?"* And, *"Why are these folks running in panicked circles?"* The past five years have shown increasingly interconnected societal and governmental exposures to these world trends as risks to our dominant culture and institutions.

From the 2024 revision of observations to our ground-level issues listing. We (all of us) face a series of conflicting, impactful, and dangerous conditions that increasingly challenge all current concepts of governance, commerce, governments, and daily human welfare. Note that these Observations may seem insurmountable problems. And that is an issue because:
These are not problems.
Problems have solutions.
These are changes in condition requiring bedrock changes in thinking without bias.
And *Change*--no matter how painful--is always the precursor to greater Opportunity.

We recommend using this list of 10 Global Factors Continuously Impeding World Stability simply as **REFERENCE POINTS** from which you may raise more specific questions concerning what in these lists may be helping or complicating positive advancements inside your own organizations.

1. Crime and Criminal Activity, (incl: Criminal Intent, Systemic Corruption and Those Who Benefit and the Global Flows of Money)
2. Human Exploitation

3. Governance and Accountability (including Dominance and Promotion of Immediate Greed Over Long-Term Sustainability, and Citizen Alienation)
4. Expanded Perpetuation of Wars & Global Nationalism (incl. Impact on What We Consider to Be Supply Chains)
5. Planetary Climate, Ecology, & Geology
6. Extreme Polarity of Wealth and Economic Survivability (incl.: the Expanding Policy Influence of Prisons and Incarceration as an Industry)
7. Technology Advancement & Speed of Communications: Ungovernable and Unmanageable Accelerating Rates of Change (including Generative AI)
8. Terrorism, Cyber Crime, and the Weapons Industries
9. Loss of Individual Personal Integrity as a Standard Leadership Prerequisite
10. Combined Healthcare Industries Worldwide: (Which covers a vast array of providers, insurers, pharmaceuticals, public & private policy, care and medical service facilities, legacy distribution systems, etc.) that will require far more simultaneous coordination design and execution to resolve.)

Bear in mind that within any such list of macro-challenges, there are always positive new solutions opportunities to be discovered!

[The full 2024 report is available by contacting The Creative Force Foundation.]

From these observation summaries, five recurring ideas emerged forming the basis of the paradoxes we must understand and assign future research before we can solve pressing issues in both business and society:

- We are experiencing times of high collateral damage to reputations, laws, and the instruments of social order.

- We have begun to replace science, facts, and law with legitimized lies, false reporting, and disinformation in several areas of the world.
- Fully mirroring George Orwell's 1949 novel *1984*, some attempt erasures of known history with de-education and new forms of 24/7 propaganda.
- There is a paradoxical rise of demanded loyalty to the PERSON rather than a nation or region or pact, accompanied by calls for conscious abandonment of previously understood common ethics and standards of universal and human excellence.
- A publicly rewarded human meanness can be often found.

None of this is completely new in human history, as recorded by Lt. Colonel (Ret) Phillips' large contribution. But here is the warning: no system of hierarchical governance has survived the convergence of these factors.

Of greater concern is a simple overview of the past 4,000 years that indicates that the duration timeline of such systems (monarchic, theocratic, authoritarian, charismatic, chartered, or otherwise) consistently shortens over time. Piasecki refers to this as cultural turbulence in his books; others refer to it as "a fracturing" rather than reintegrating. This fracturing into opposing fragments proceeds as:

- Technology advances
- Communications advances
- Lifespans increase
- Natural interventions or catastrophes occur like severe weather

With some consternation, we have noted that over such histories, four phenomena also consistently proved unsustainable:

- Choosing an ill-defined and "contrived" future direction
- Repeated attempts to return to an imagined past

- Hero worship or "cult of personality" stemming from power or greed, accompanied by authoritarian exemptions from direct accountability
- Expanding fractures within the roles of religions across the globe, such as in Buddhism, Christian, Hindu, Judaic, Muslim, and other regions.

<u>Noted with some concern</u>: Cultures that appear to have experienced any two of these four phenomena went into societal remission, thus becoming highly vulnerable to multiple forms of aggression.

What appears unique today is not simply that this is happening, so much as the relentless confluence with which such actions are being deliberately deployed and are simultaneously increasing. Match these checklists against your own tactical and strategic thinking.

Concluding Context for this Anthology

We did not write this book lightly. This version represents the fifth revision of our ground-level observations on global trends and patterns. We all recognize a series of conflicting, impactful, and dangerous conditions that increasingly challenge all current concepts of governance, commerce, governments, and daily human welfare.

Let this serve to suggest and open the door to (a.) new and more rigorous and specifically applied research efforts while (b.) encouraging the practitioner, enterprise owner, executive and professional manager to dig further for the solutions & opportunities that will be discovered and applied.

Over the past 30+ years, a few of us have issued standing lists of the top issues we see impacting the world. These two recent lists more narrowly focus on risks and exposures that:

- **have already converged**
- are **now accelerating,**
- offer **present clear and present dangers**
- **cannot now be reversed** by present common thinking, behaviors, approaches, etc. We need new organizing frames of mind and action.

We recommend using these chapters as **reference points** from which you may raise more specific questions concerning what may be helping or complicating positive advancements inside your own organizations. For professionals, practitioners, and executives, such factors will include, but will not be limited to: clients, markets, affected populations, countries, suppliers, employees, competitors, government(s), organizations, factions, and criminal enterprises.

The Fundamental Takeaways in 2025

While governance is a critical issue in navigating your institution through these minefields, be clear that leading by "actually deciding to lead" continues as a critical and ongoing challenge. Use the chapters on governance, accounting, supply chain, and education to rethink who and how the decision-makers must now need to be better prepared.

Using our observation protocols, all my summary observations are vetted against each of the following:

- **It is global**
- **It impacts everything you will do**
- **It has already begun**
- **It is inescapable**

Remember! You *Always* Hold the Power to Make Positive Change

These trends may seem frightening, but every one of us has Four Great Powers, outlined at the beginning of this book, to effect positive change.

- The power to convene
- The power to observe
- The power to believe
- The power to choose to do good

How does one use these powers? Just as I described to the students, faculty, and guests during the 2012 Bentley University speech honoring Martin Luther King Jr., excerpted and adapted here:

"The power of the individual to do good and to make changes and to accomplish those changes and to help and to heal is the most unrealized, unexploited, unrecognized power on earth. Open your eyes and see the opportunities. Open your eyes and dream what is possible. If you want to change the world, it is so easy to be terribly overwhelmed by the destruction, suffering, poverty, and disease. The list goes on and on. But there is something you can do. Save one child. Save one child! All the gold on earth does not equal looking into the face of a parent whose child you have saved ... and you have That. Absolute. Power!"

Collectively, we hope this helps your work and your impact.

Darryl Vernon Poole, August 2024

Appendix:

Top 90 World Trends Books at Your Side - a Short Further Readings 'Crash List'

Works helping to inform our collective "Sense of the Near Future" as Selected over a 50-Year period by D.V. Poole.

Ackerman (Elliot) and Stavros (James, Admiral); **2034: A Novel of the Next World War**, Penguin Press, 2021.

Adams-Ender, Clara L. (BG, U.S. Army, Ret.) with Walker, Blair S.; **My Rise to the Stars: How a Sharecropper's Daughter Became an Army General**, CAPE Assocs., Inc., 2001.

Anderson, Elijah; **BLACK IN WHITE SPACE: the Enduring Impact of Color in Everyday Life**, University of Chicago Press, 2022.

Archer, James, **THE PLOT TO SEIZE THE WHITE HOUSE**, Skyhorse Publishing, 2015.

Antoninus, Marcus Aurelius; **MEDITATIONS**, Penguin Classics, 2006 (original written:170-180c.e., Richard Graves translation:1792).

Baker, Raymond W.; **INVISIBLE TRILLIONS: How Financial Secrecy Is Imperiling Capitalism and Democracy—and the Way to Renew Our Broken System**, Barre& Koehler, 2023.

Beitzel, Barry J., et al.; **BIBLICA: THE BIBLE ATLAS | *A Social and Historical Journey Through the Lands of the Bible***, Barrons

Educational Services, 2007 (orig. Global Book Publishing, Pty Ltd., 2006).

Bogle, John C.; **ENOUGH: True Measures of Money, Business, and Life**, John Wiley and Sons, 2007.

Brockett, Ann and Rezaee, Zabihollah; **CORPORATE SUSTAINABILITY: Integrating Performance and Reporting**, John Wiley & Sons, Inc., 2012 (Axiom Gold Award in Business Ethics, 2013).

Brose, Christian; **THE KILL CHAIN: Defending America in the Future of High-Tech Warfare**, Hatchette Books, 2020.

Buckley, William F., Jr.; **MILES GONE BY: A Literary Autobiography**, Regnery Publishing, 2004.

Butler, Smedley D., Brigadier General; War Is a Racket (w/additional Butler essays, introduction by Adam Parfrey, photos from 'the Horror of It' by Frederick A. Barber), Butler Family, 1935-1939 and Feral House (all combined), 2003.

Carson, Rachel; **SILENT SPRING**, Houghton Mifflin, 1962.

Coates, Ta-Nehisi; **BETWEEN THE WORLD AND ME**, Spiegel & Grau, 2015.

Deming, W. Edward; **THE ESSENTIAL DEMING: Leadership Principles form the Father of Quality**, *Edited by Joyce Nilsson Orsini, Ph.D.*, McGraw Hill, 2013.

Dickens, Charles; **A CHRISTMAS CAROL IN PROSE, BEING A GHOST STORY OF CHRISTMAS**, Chapman and Hall, 1843.

Drucker, Peter F.; MANAGEMENT: Tasks, Responsibilities, Practices; Harper Collins, 1974.

Eco, Umberto; THE NAME OF THE ROSE, The Folio Society, 2001

Ehrenreich, Barbara; NICKEL AND DIMED: On (Not) Getting By in America *(20th Anniversary Edition)*, Metropolitan Books, Henry Holt and Co., 2023 (orig. 2001).

Fischer, David Hackett; AFRICAN FOUNDERS: How Enslaved People Expanded American Ideals, Simon & Schuster, 2022.

Forrester, Daniel Patrick; CONSIDER: Harnessing the Power of Reflective Thinking in Your Organization, WILLCHAR Press, 2nd ed, 2021.

Franklin, John Hop;: MIRROR TO AMERICA: the Autobiography of John Hope Franklin, Farrar, Straus and Giroux; 2005.

Friedman, Milton; CAPITALISM AND FREEDOM, University of Chicago, 2020 (with 1982 and 2002 reissue Prefaces by author and new Forward by Benjamin Applebaum) (Orig. 1962).

Goldratt, Eliyahu M. with Cox, Jeff; THE GOAL: a Process of Ongoing Improvement, North River Press, 2014.

Great Spiritual Books, *Choose the principal guiding text of your choice from 11 of the greater referenced:* (Holy Qur'An or Koran, the Four Books of Shia Islam, the Holy Bible complete with all 'lost books,' Bhagavad Gita, Tripitaka, Holy Vedas, Upanishads, Four Books and Five Classics of Confucius, Tao Te Ching, Talmud including both Babylonian and Jerusalem teachings, and the Kojiki); *multiple authors and publishers, sourced in C.E., pre-C.E. histories; and* antiquity.

Haire, Mason (Ed.); **Modern Organization Theory**, John Wiley, 1959.

Hammurabi, **Code of Hammurabi**, Babylonian Kingdom during period of 1792-1750 b.c.e., (modern versions are widely independently published).

Hayek, Friedrich A., **Law, Legislation and Liberty** [Volume 2: **the Mirage of Social Justice**], Phoenix | the University of Chicago Press, 1976.

Henson, Josiah; **Uncle Tom's Story of His Life: An Autobiography of the Rev. Josiah Henson**, Adams & Madison Press, 2019. Original Pub.: 1858, Ontario, Canada.

Hill (Linda A.), Brandeau (Greg), Truelove (Emily), and Lineback (Jent); **Collective Genius: the Art and Practice of Leading Innovation**, Harvard Business Review Press, 2014.

Howe, Neil; **the Fourth turning is Here**, Simon & Schuster, 2023. (Updates William Strauss and Neil Howe's original 1997 book, **the Fourth Turning: an American Prophecy**).

Ialen., Vincent; **Deep Time Reckoning**, MIT Press, 2020.

Jones, Robert P.; **the Hidden Roots of White Supremacy and the Path to a Shared American Future**, Simon & Schuster, 2023.

Juran, Joseph M., and Gryna, Frank M.; **Juran's Quality Control Handbook - 4th Edition**, McGraw-Hill, 1988.

Kahneman (Daniel), Sibony (Olivier), Sunstein (Cass R.); **Noise: A Flaw in Human Judgement**, Little Brown Spark, 2021.

Kagan, Donald; ON THE ORIGINS OF WAR, Doubleday, 1995.

Kahneman, Daniel; THINKING, FAST AND SLOW, Farrar, Straus, and Giroux, 2011.

Keys, David; CATASTROPHE, Ballantine, 2000.

King, Martin Luther, Jr.; *LETTER FROM BIRMINGHAM CITY JAIL*, American Friends Service Committee, 1963.

Knoke, William; **BOLD NEW WORLD: the Essential Road Map to the Twenty-First Century**, Kodansha International, 1996.

Krugman, Paul R.; **THE ACCIDENTAL THEORIST: and Other Dispatches from the Dismal Science**, W. W. Norton & Co., 1998.

Müller, Ingo; **HITLER'S JUSTICE: the Courts of the Third Reich**, (trans: Deborah Lucas Schneider), Harvard University, 1991.

Musashi, Miyamoto (*formal name:* Shinmen Musashi-no-Kami Fujiwara no Harunobi); THE BOOK OF FIVE RINGS, 1645 (modern versions are widely independently published).

Nordhaus, William D.; **THE SPIRIT OF GREEN: the Economics of Collisions and Contagions in a Crowded World**, Princeton University Press, 2021.

Orwell, George *(pen name used by: Eric Arthur Blair)*; NINETEEN EIGHTY-FOUR *(a.k.a.:* **1984**), Secker & Warburg, 1949 *(since published by many global independent presses).*

Perry, Imani; SOUTH TO AMERICA, Harper Collins, 2022.

Piasecki, Bruce W.; **WEALTH AND CLIMATE COMPETITIVENESS: The New Narrative on Business and Society**, Rodin Press (2024) and **WORLD, INC.**, Sourcebooks, 2007.

Porter, Michael E.; **COMPETITIVE STRATEGY**, Free Press, 1980 and **COMPETITIVE ADVANTAGE**, Free Press, 1985.

Press, Eyal; **BEAUTIFUL SOULS: Saying No, Breaking Ranks, and Heeding the Voice of Conscience in Dark Times**, Farrar, Straus and Giroux, 2012.

Reinhart, Carmen M. and Rogoff, Kenneth S.; **THIS TIME IS DIFFERENT: Eight Centuries of Financial Folly**; Princeton University Press, 2009.

Rezaee, Zabihollah; **THE SUSTAINABLE BUSINESS BLUEPRINT: Planning, Performance, Risk, Reporting, and Assurance**, Routledge Taylor & Francis Group, *September 2024 (for 2025)*; **BUSINESS SUSTAINABILITY: Profit-with-Focus Purpose**, Business Expert Press, 2021 (*with* Harvard Business Publishing co-distribution, 2022).

Samuelson, Paul; **ECONOMICS [9th Edition]**, McGraw-Hill, 1973.

Sinek, Simon; **LEADERS EAT LAST: Why some Teams Pull Together and Others Don't**; Penguin Group; New York, NY; 2014 and **START WITH WHY: How Great Leaders Inspire Everyone to Take Action**, Penguin Group, 2009.

Smil, Vaclav; **NUMBERS DON'T LIE: 71 Stories to Help Us Understand the Modern World**, Penguin Books, 2020.

Snyder, Timothy; **ON TYRANNY: Twenty Lessons From the Twentieth Century**, Crown, 2017.

SPEECHES THAT CHANGED THE WORLD, *(introduction by Montefiore, Simon Sebag)*; Metro Books, 2013.

Stanley, Jason; HOW FASCISM WORKS: The Politics of US and THEM, Random House, 2018.

Sun, Tzu (Wu); THE ART OF WAR, 5th Century BC; (confirmed by: 1972 discovery of Han tombs containing the Yinqueshan Han Slips).

Sussman, Robert Wald; THE MYTH OF Race: the Troubling Persistence of an Unscientific Idea, Harvard University Press, 2014.

Taleb, Nassim; SKIN IN THE GAME, Random House, 2020 and THE BLACK SWAN: the Impact of the Highly Improbable, Random House, 2007.

Terkel, Louis "Studs"; WORKING (People Talk About What They Do All Day and How They Feel About What They Do), The New Press, 1997.

Thomas, Lewis; THE LIVES OF A CELL: Notes of a Biology Watcher, Penguin Books, 1974 *(reissued, 1978)*.

Tuckman, Barbara W.; A DISTANT MIRROR: the Calamitous Fourteenth Century, Random House, 1978 (1987 pb). and THE GUNS OF AUGUST, Macmillan, 1962.

Tufte, Edward R.; THE VISUAL DISPLAY OF QUANTITATIVE INFORMATION (2nd ed.), Graphics Press, 2001 (orig. 1983) and POLITICAL CONTROL OF THE ECONOMY, Princeton University Press, 1978.

Ury, William; GETTING PAST NO: Negotiating with Difficult People, Bantam Books, 1991.

Vague, Richard; **the Paradox of Debt: A New Path to Prosperity Without Crisis**, UPenn Press, 2023.

Walter, Barbara; **How Civil Wars Start And How to Stop Them**, Crown, 2022.

Washington, George, et al. (with Alexander Hamilton, 1792, and James Madison, 1796) ; **Farwell Address (to Friends and Citizens)**, delivered on September 17, 1796, and Published on September 19, 1796.

Weitz, John; **Hitler's Banker: Hjalmar Horace Greeley Schacht**, Little, Brown and Company, 1997.

Wheeler, Keith; **Peaceable Lane**, Simon & Schuster (orig.), January 1, 1960, Signet (pb), April 7, 2012.

Winestone, Ted; **Run to the Woods: A Journey from Survival to Triumph**, Captain Ted Publishing; Germantown TN; 2020.

Wishard, William Van Dusen; **Between Two Ages: The 21st Century and the Crisis of Meaning**; Xlibris Corp. (original:2000, pb:2003).

Woodson, Carter G.; the Mis-Education of the Negro; Penguin Books. 2017 (original:1933, pb 2023).

Yergin, Daniel H. ; **the New Map: Energy, Climate, and the Clash of Nations**; Penguin Books (original:2020, pb:2021).

Limited Endnotes

Critical World Trends and Combined Cultural Power: What Experts Are Finding Out About the Near Future

Chapter #4

1   Clay – (https://sdgs.un.org/goals)

2   Clay - Vaughan, F. (2002). What is spiritual intelligence? *Journal of Humanistic Psychology, 42*(2), 16–33.

Chapter #5

3   Eater - (https://www.themyersbriggs.com/en-US/Programs/Conflict-at-Work-Research)

4   Easter - (https://www.who.int/news-room/fact-sheets/detail/mental-health-at-work)

5   Easter - (https://news.gallup.com/poll/270296/americans-dislike-big-business.aspx)

6   Easter - (https://linktr.ee/creator-report)

7   Easter - (https://streamhatchet.com/reports/)

8   Easter - (https://insights.streamhatchet.com/the-creator-mental-health-report#:~:text=Digital%20Creators%20are%20burning%20out,and%20lesser%20quality%20of%20life)

9   Story - Esper, Terry L., et al. "Everything old is new again: The age of consumer-centric supply chain management." *Journal of Business Logistics* 41.4 (2020): 286-293.

10 Story - Typically defined as students that are above traditional college age (24) and/or have other life characteristics such as a full-time job, children, or residence circumstances (among other variables) that can interfere with the completion of educational objectives.

11 Story – (https://www.aboutamazon.com/news/workplace/our-upskilling-2025-programs)

12   Story - (https://www.marketplace.org/2024/07/17/a-look-at-part-of-amazons-1-2-billion-on-the-job-training-investment/)

13   Story - (https://stories.starbucks.com/stories/2023/starbucks-furthers-commitment-to-sustainable-dairy/)

14   Story - (https://content-prod-live.cert.starbucks.com/binary/v2/asset/137-88758.pdf)

15   Story - (https://www.inditex.com/itxcomweb/api/media/2f896a99-1b0f-4757-8242-3256e1701cee/Supply_chain_management_transform_sector.pdf?t=1716284533068)